Advance Praise for
Come Back to Bed

Retail is not dead. At Gallery Furniture, we live by the principles Mark and Mark have laid out. We are fearless promoters, live to serve our customers, and know the importance of being different. This book is a must-read for retailers who want to go from surviving to thriving.

—Jim "Mattress Mack" McIngvale, Owner, Gallery Furniture

Mark Quinn and Mark Kinsley provide a uniquely practical and relevant perspective to mattress retailing. Their principles are remarkably timely to how retailers can adapt in this COVID-impacted environment. *Come Back to Bed* is an optimistic, progressive book that leverages their industry knowledge in an engaging way and is useful to anyone in the category.

—Steve Rusing, EVP and President of US Sales,
Tempur Sealy International

When you first hear about it, an all-mattress podcast sounds a little crazy. But Mark Quinn and Mark Kinsley have created something with *Dos Marcos* that's interesting, intriguing, irreverent, insightful, and downright fun. *Come Back to Bed* builds on that legacy. It showcases the people and principles that make America's independent retailers unique and offers all small-business owners, regardless of product category, the tools they need to help differentiate themselves from national chains and own their local markets.

—Tom Hickman, President and Chief Member Advocate,
Nationwide Marketing Group

The guiding principles found in *Come Back to Bed* are invaluable for any retailer or entrepreneur striving to create that "noticeable difference" in every aspect of their business. Mark and Mark have filled these pages with golden nuggets just waiting to be found by those willing to dig.

—**Harry Roberts, Co-founder, Mattress Firm**

The two Marks, Quinn and Kinsley, have significant insight into the fascinating world of mattress retail. They identify the good, the bad, and the ugly. Most importantly, they offer solutions. The book is a must-read, but only for those who want to be successful and do it the right way!

—**Karl Glassman, Chairman and CEO, Leggett & Platt**

The *Dos Marcos* guys are truly students of retail and marketing. They have studied success stories across the industry and helped capture best practices that can truly benefit everyone!

—**Peter Bolton, Chief Operating Officer, Jordan's**

Dos Marcos delivers the steak—a bevy of business-building insights—and the sizzle—including appearances by Bigfoot, prizefighters, and zany mattress characters, of which they are two notable examples. This book is a fantastic follow-up to their show, which really is the galaxy's greatest mattress podcast and a treat for all of us on Earth to enjoy.

—**David Perry, Executive Editor, *Furniture Today***

Mark and Mark have such a passion for the mattress business it's infectious. They are true Mattress Geeks when it comes to products, the consumer experience, consumer feedback, and most importantly, the retail sales associates. They love this business and are always looking for ways to help others grow.

—**Bill Papettas, President, Mattress Warehouse**

COME
BACK
TO BED

COME BACK TO BED

ATTRACT MORE

FOOT TRAFFIC

AND MAKE PEOPLE

FALL IN LOVE

WITH YOUR STORE

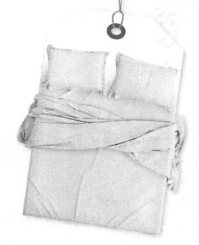

MARK KINSLEY *and* MARK QUINN

LIONCREST
PUBLISHING

COME BACK TO BED
Attract More Foot Traffic and Make People Fall in Love with Your Store

ISBN   978-1-5445-1730-8 *Hardcover*
          978-1-5445-1731-5 *Paperback*
          978-1-5445-1732-2 *Ebook*
          978-1-5445-1789-6 *Audiobook*

Contents

Foreword

I met Mark Quinn and Mark Kinsley through an email. A leader of our furniture and bedding division at Nationwide Marketing Group sent over a proposed sponsorship opportunity for, I kid you not, "the Galaxy's Greatest Mattress Podcast." At the time, I was responsible for overseeing Nationwide's PR efforts, so I was excited to see a new media option in the industry. I also feared that many in the business might not be entirely engaged in the wave of folks who had deserted terrestrial radio and embraced the wonderful world of podcasting. However, always open to hear out those who are blazing their own paths, I enthusiastically agreed to take a call with the two Marks, or the Dos Marcos.

In minutes, I knew they were both "one of us."

In my two decades in retail, I've learned three lessons that have held fast. First, to truly succeed in business (and in life), you must be different in the way you think, the actions you take, and the way you lead. Second, you must care more about the success of others than about your own. And third, to accomplish those first two, you'll need comrades who see the importance of both. That third lesson has impacted my career as much as or more than the first two. It quickly became evident that discovering those like-minded folks was easy and natural, even though their numbers may be small. In short, you've got to be one of us in order to find the rest of us.

That planned introductory call, scheduled for thirty minutes, lasted over two hours, and there I found two of "us." Mark and Mark's energy, innovative thinking, courage to be radically different, and true servants' hearts were captivating. It's tribal: your vibe will always attract your tribe, and for those who are passionate about succeeding in retail and doing it the right way, you want Quinn and Kinsley in your tribe. This book will provide all the evidence of that you'll need. I can't imagine my own tribe today without Quinn and Kinsley.

Since that initial meeting, I've gotten to know both Marks on a personal and professional level. The Dos Marcos dynamic duo has appeared at three consecutive Nationwide PrimeTime events (the industry's largest convention and buying show for independent retailers) headlining Mattress University, and each time, they've raised the bar. They're forever innovating, forever challenging the status quo, forever summoning the courage to try new things. Both Quinn and Kinsley have credentials that are unquestioned in the mattress industry, as both have been thought leaders in the space since before that term entered business jargon. However, their passion, ideas, and insights apply far beyond their home industry. No matter what business you're in, if the key to your success lies in attracting, serving, and retaining consumers, this book is for you. The question isn't whether you'll find a great idea here—it's how many you'll discover and how greatly they'll enhance your success.

I'm forever grateful for the collaboration, the wisdom and guidance, and most of all, the friendship of Quinn and Kinsley. As you turn these pages, you're in for quite a ride! So buckle up, get ready, and gather 'round the campfire! Even if you come with just a few small sticks, the pages that follow are filled with sparks, and your own roaring flame of success will quickly follow.

Mike Whitaker
Nationwide Marketing Group

Bringing Customers to Your Bed

The founder of Mattress Firm, Harry Roberts, knocked on the door to the greenroom. We were dressed head-to-toe in milk-white clothes. The gold chains draped around our necks were encrusted in fake diamonds forming the words "Springz" and "Phoam."

After hugs and high fives, Harry reached into his bag and pulled out a paper sack with three tequila shooters. "Cheers," we said as we threw back the Don Julio and sucked limes.

In 1986, Harry and his college buddies Paul Stork and Steve Fendrich founded Mattress Firm, a bedding store that would become the largest sleep-shop chain in the United States. A mattress industry legend, Harry had swung by the Houston Convention Center to make good on a promise.

A few months prior, Harry was a guest on the *Dos Marcos* podcast. It's a show hosted by us, Mark Quinn and Mark Kinsley, that's dedicated to the mattress industry. We recorded a two-part special where Harry told stories about the early days of Mattress Firm and how the founders clawed their way to the top.

We had a blast recording. Harry promised if we visited Houston, tequila shots were on him. Our nerves were running high, so that tequila came at a good time.

More than four hundred mattress retailers were waiting for Dos Marcos to take the stage. We were speaking at Nationwide Marketing Group's PrimeTime event. The topic of the speech was "How to Drive Big Foot Traffic."

Neither of us operates retail stores, and we were about to tell a room full of owners, and industry titan Harry Roberts, how to get more people to walk through their doors.

So yeah, that tequila came at a good time.

The number one challenge facing independent mattress retailers is getting consumers to visit their stores. People can't fall in love with your store if they don't visit it. In the age of online shopping and endless options, many mom-and-pop shops are withering and dying, or searching for creative ways to stay relevant. We wanted to help this audience by offering creative ideas on how to attract store traffic.

Even though we had recorded more than 140 podcast episodes, the event in Houston was only the second speech we'd ever co-delivered. We were nervous as hell. Not because we were speaking in front of a large group, but because we were about to do something completely out of our comfort zone. Even for us, it was wild.

The white outfits and rappers' chains were all part of the show opener, a rap song performance that involved Bigfoot, the beast's handler, and a man in a dress.

For us, it was important we "bring the thunder" because a large part of our speech focused on pushing retailers to find ways to be different and meaningfully connect to consumers.

Be bold. Grab attention. Stand out in your marketplace. Capture the hearts and minds of your audience. That was the crux of our message. Since we were preaching that gospel, we wanted to live it.

We also knew the content of our speech must be relevant and useful. Once we'd captured the attention of our audience, we were going to tell them how to thrive in the rocky, shifting mattress industry.

The bedding business changed dramatically between 2010 and 2020. With the growth of e-commerce and the increased cost and complexity of advertising, retail store traffic dropped significantly. Instead of accepting the change or relapsing into old habits, we wanted retailers to crack that eggshell and emerge as a big bad chicken, ready to take on the foxes and coyotes.

To kick off the speech, Jeff Rose from Nationwide introduced Dos Marcos. Then our friends Chad Fischer and Johnny Lamp emerged from a side door. Johnny Lamp was dressed up as Bigfoot. Acting as his handler, Chad lured Bigfoot to the stage with a bag of beef jerky.

Bigfoot took his place next to the turntable, put on his headphones, and dropped the beat, launching a mattress rap video that splashed across three massive screens.

Dressed like hip-hop stars with sunglasses and gold chains, we busted open the back door and started dancing down the center aisle, rapping with the song, high-fiving people in the audience, and praying we didn't screw up.

In our experience, every rap video has an attractive female lead. We couldn't find one. Instead, our tattooed, goateed, ex-Marine friend Mike Whitaker put on a purple dress from Grandma's closet and crushed the chorus.

The energy in the room went from a two to a ten. We sang and danced. We executed most of the choreography, had a blast in the process, and gave our audience something to talk about for the rest of the show. Mission accomplished.

Times Have Changed—for Good

In early 2020, before COVID-19 fast-tracked the retail apocalypse, Art Van, a large Michigan-based furniture and mattress chain announced it was filing for bankruptcy and shutting down all 169 locations. In January of 2019, Kentucky-based Innovative Mattress Solutions, operators of 142 sleep shops, filed for bankruptcy. Mattress Firm filed Chapter 11 in October of 2018 and closed seven hundred stores.

The retail horror story that began before the coronavirus goes on and on. Gap stores gone. Macy's melted. Sears sank. Bed Bath and Beyond—bye-bye to more than forty stores. Thirty-two Lucky's Markets weren't so lucky. Kmart (yes, there were still some around) couldn't compete. GameStop suffered more than three hundred store closings, and arts and crafts store A.C. Moore shuttered all of its 145 stores.

Then the new coronavirus began infecting people around the globe. COVID-19 spread from country to country and person to person, killing hundreds of thousands along the way. The human race was forced to fight a global pandemic and, in the process, figure out how to recover in a decimated economy. One day we were going about normal life with unemployment at all-time lows. Days later we were staying home, no longer shopping or eating out, and isolating ourselves.

Still, while store closures captured national headlines, thousands of independent retailers remained afloat. They were bobbing in the ocean, clinging to a plank of wood splintered from the hull of a sunken ship, but they were alive. And their optimistic spirit told them land was near.

The pain that pierced retailers was almost unbearable. For many, it was more than they could endure. They didn't make it. For those who kept swimming and soon found land, the fight to stay alive has continued.

They've washed ashore on an island that resembles home. But the rules have changed. Customers are different. Expectations for retailers have changed. Fearing these changes, many of these castaways will leave the island, brave the sea, and search for a safer, more familiar place to call home. Others will master the rules, move forward, and spend no time thinking, "I wish it would all go back to how it was."

There's no going back to the way it was. Our old home has disappeared into the sea. We're on a new island, and it's time to screw your head on straight and *do the work* it takes to thrive here.

The Making of *Dos Marcos*

In 2011, Mark Quinn was the Segment Vice President of Marketing for the Home Furnishings Group at Leggett & Platt and Mark Kinsley was Vice President for a marketing firm, MediaCross, headquartered in St. Louis. Kinsley led the team for the Leggett account, and after working together for a year, Quinn hired Kinsley to come to work at Leggett & Platt as the Vice President of Marketing for the Bedding Group.

The job change put the two Marks together full-time, creating marketing programs, increasing Leggett's visibility in the mattress industry, and eventually starting the *Dos Marcos* podcast, "the Galaxy's Greatest Mattress Podcast."

Quinn eventually left Leggett to start his own bedding company called Spink and Co., a farm-to-bedroom luxury mattress producer. In 2019, Kinsley became President and

CEO of Englander, a top-ten mattress producer with licensees in twenty-eight countries at the time.

Through it all, Mark and Mark continued producing the *Dos Marcos* podcast. That platform became a campfire around which mattress industry leaders gather to tell stories, share ideas, build relationships, and highlight amazing people who fill this $16 billion industry with life.

We see the industry from a unique angle because, through the podcast and through our leadership roles in mattress companies, we engage with suppliers, manufacturers, retailers, and retail sales associates.

Our companies touch thousands of retail doors. That affords us a glimpse into a huge number of businesses. Even though we don't own retail stores, our relationships with so many companies have given us the opportunity to identify themes and spot patterns.

Imagine you're on that new island and you take a walk. Hacking your way through the jungle, you come to a clearing and see two guys. That's us. We're cracking jokes, feeding the monkeys bananas, and playing games with the native kids. We don't have everything figured out, but we are comfortable in this strange new world. We're not scared to try and fail. We've learned our way around. And we're here to be your guides.

What You'll Learn

This book is not about the basics. It's about taking the basics and building a brand around those ideas. If you cannot dribble a basketball, you will not win the game. This book does not teach you how to dribble.

The fundamentals of the mattress business are merchandising, sales, service, and delivery. This book is not focused on product selection, selling techniques, operations, or training. We will not be talking about comfort guarantees, warranties, or closing techniques. This book is not filled with price and promotion advertising ideas—the heroin of the mattress industry. We repeat: this book is not about furniture promotions or tent sales. Inside these pages, you will not find quick-hit ideas for driving foot traffic.

There are many books that focus on Facebook marketing or TikTok tactics. They promise to make you an influencer, a marketing expert, or a Google AdWords ninja. This is not one of those books. It does not dive deeply into tactics. Tactics change.

This book focuses on principles and strategies, which apply regardless of time and place. Tactics are sticks that break when you bend them too hard. Principles are flexible like ropes that can be knotted and tied and used to tow a truck or climb a mountain. Ropes aren't rigid, so they're useful in a variety of situations. The principles and strategies we offer are based on observations, conversations, and research. There are some opinions, but we use evidence to back up our ideas.

At its heart, this book is about finding the soul of your business and celebrating what makes you different. It's about finding the right chord to strike so you connect with consumers on a deep level and build relationships that will last a lifetime. Absent value, people make decisions on price—*especially if they don't know you.* This book pushes you to find your brand and build value in everything you sell and in all you do. This is your key to bringing customers back to bed.

We're writing this book for the mattress industry. It's our love letter to a special business and the remarkable people who fill it. But these ideas work whether you're an independent retailer selling furniture and flooring or shoes and apparel. You might sell dog treats, tires, health food, jewelry, or flowers. Maybe you're struggling to build an identity around your appliance business, or you run a restaurant that needs a refresh. Chiropractors, dentists, and doctors all need to prove they're different. Spas, gyms, beauty salons, and barbershops must stand out to compete. Community banks and car dealers need help. If you run a business, this book will help you discover principles for building a brand that's *notorious* in your marketplace.

A post-coronavirus economy doesn't affect the framework for creating a brand, positioning your business, and developing a strong message. If you work through this book and the world goes through another shift, the teachings should still apply. Regardless of how the world changes, you'll gain the knowledge and know-how to reframe your business and put yourself back on the path to success.

If you're stuck, we're going to show you how to blast that logjam with dynamite. We argue that *deciding to do things differently* is critical to your future. Your ability to connect with people dictates the health of your business. We'll outline the reasons for investing in building a brand and how to position your business in a way that makes you number one in your marketplace. You'll discover a method for generating creative ideas that anyone can deploy. Finally, we'll explain how to push your ads, assets, marketing, brand, promotions, and ideas into the world and attract more foot traffic.

Inside these pages you'll read rich examples from real business owners operating on the front lines, people who have been kind enough to share their stories to help you. You'll read about Greg and Katy Law, owners of Sweet Dreams Mattress and Furniture in Lake Norman, North Carolina. The Sweet Dreams brand is dedicated to *making everyone's dreams come true,* and they live out that mission in creative and fun ways—they even have a superhero named Mattman (aka Andrew Schlesser) who's been recognized by the local chamber of commerce.

You'll meet Trent Ranburger. His creative, foot-traffic-generating TV commercials have been featured on a list of the world's dumbest commercials and his business, Trent Bedding, has been named Best of Bowling Green, Kentucky, ten years running. We want to shine a light on positivity in the mattress industry, learn from others, and share what we've discovered. Along the way, we want to have a lot of fun and inspire people to be their best.

You might not feel ready to change. If that's the case, you may discover important concepts, but you won't put them into practice. Remember, when the student is ready, the teacher appears. If you're ready, read on. And if you're not ready to change, read on anyway. Action is the answer. Begin a journey that leads to a place of readiness.

The first step is looking at the past and gaining perspective. You need to understand some mattress history, learn from it, and become enlightened about the forces shaping the world in which we live.

Chapter One

State of the Mattress Industry

E ven before COVID-19, few industries had been more disrupted than the mattress business.

For decades, people shopping for a mattress visited a retail store. They'd test a few beds, pay for the mattress, strap that white rectangle to the top of their station wagon, and head home.

The business model for mattresses stayed constant because beds are bulky and hard to move. Manufacturers would ship products to a retailer's warehouse, and retailers would sell to consumers, who hauled the mattress home or had it delivered. There weren't many ways to skip a step.

Until compressed mattresses came along.

In terms of industries e-commerce has massively disrupted, books and beds are both near the top of the list.

Amazon began selling books online in 1995 and has since wiped out major brick-and-mortar retailers. Few people would have imagined the fate of books and beds would collide. Today,

Amazon is the number one seller of books and *roll-packed mattresses* in the United States.

To roll-pack a mattress, you place it into a machine that compresses it, folds it, and rolls it like a burrito. The mattress is shipped in a box about the size of a mini fridge. Shippers like UPS or FedEx deliver the mattress to a consumer's front door. They unroll it, cut the plastic seal, and voilà, the mattress expands back to life and fully recovers in about twenty-four hours.

While working at Leggett & Platt, the world's largest manufacturer of mattress innersprings and bedding components, we often pondered this question: What component technology would disrupt springs? Was there a support system that could be produced at scale that would swallow innersprings and send the industry in a new direction? Few people thought innovations in mattress compression, packaging, and shipping would forever alter the coastline of mattress country.

A company called BedInABox was an early pioneer in selling compressed mattresses online. The BedInABox.com website says, "In the fall of 2004, a foam expert, a digital marketer and a machine builder with a wild idea got together in Johnson City, Tennessee, to discuss the concept of putting a queen size mattress into a box that the freight companies would accept. Eighteen months later an industry was born from the imagination and leadership of Bill Bradley, the creator of that first machine used to put a BedInABox."

Even though BedInABox introduced the concept of shippable mattresses, Tuft & Needle took it to a new level.

JT Marino and Daehee Park launched Tuft & Needle in 2012 shortly after JT and his wife endured a frustrating mattress-shopping experience. At the time, Park and Marino were Penn State graduates working in Silicon Valley. The duo was looking to start a business in an industry whose consumers hated their shopping experience. Traditional mattress retail was known for slimy salespeople and a confusing process. JT and Daehee created a list of things they disliked about mattress shopping, and from that *hate list*, Tuft & Needle was born.

Then came Casper, a money-raising, brand-building juggernaut that followed Tuft & Needle into the online mattress retail business. Casper raised millions of dollars from big-name investors like Leonardo DiCaprio, 50 Cent, and Ashton Kutcher. Kylie Jenner even posted a picture of her new Casper mattress that got 870,000 likes on Instagram. With all this attention, the brand generated $1.8 million in sales in its first two months.

Online upstarts understood the shift to a consumer-centric world. Their founders felt the pain customers experienced when shopping for a mattress. By limiting selection and creating a convenient way to shop, they drew adoring fans to mattress websites that promised better sleep at a better price, shipped to your door.

Soon after Tuft & Needle and Casper launched their perfect mattress business model, the floodgates for look-alikes and imitators burst. Brands like Nectar, Saatva, Leesa, and Purple entered the roll-pack mattress space. The list of newbies mushroomed from a dozen or so startups to more than 175 online brands in less than seven years. All this awareness and advertising around mattresses came at a time when people's attitudes toward sleep were changing.

Shifting Feelings about Sleep

At 2:39 a.m. on Thursday, January 4, 2018, an earthquake struck near the historic Claremont Hotel in Berkeley, California. The

4.4 magnitude temblor shook the San Francisco Bay Area and jolted people awake.

Developers working at Fitbit received a flood of data from people wearing fitness-tracking devices. When the earthquake rumbled through Berkeley, the number of people awake jumped from 8 percent to 52 percent.

Farther from the epicenter of the quake, data showed more people stayed asleep.

While seismologists likely found the data useful, those following the sleep space saw something else unfolding. For the first time in history on any large scale, human beings got a glimpse of what happens during the one-third of their lives spent asleep. That glimpse into the unknown, even if the data wasn't entirely accurate, may have sparked an interest in and basic understanding of sleep.

It's common knowledge that we need to eat right, sleep right, and exercise in order to live our best life. We can measure our diet with a scale, we can quantify the benefit of exercise as we lift more and run farther, but when it comes to sleep the feedback is mostly subjective. As Kinsley's Grandma Minnie used to say when asked how she slept, "I'm not sure. I didn't stay awake to find out."

Back to the earthquake and fitness trackers. Early Fitbits only measured movement. To accurately measure sleep quality, researchers monitor breathing rate, heart rate, and body temperature. So that Fitbit data wasn't 100 percent accurate. But that's not the point. For the first time ever, people had quantifiable data attached to sleep, and they became interested in getting better rest.

Politicians and business leaders have often worn their *lack of needing sleep* as a badge of honor. The "I don't need sleep" attitudes are slowly disappearing as those who spent their lives getting by on less than six hours begin to develop dementia. Yes, lack of sleep is now shown to be a *cause* of Alzheimer's.

As people stare at Fitbit data and listen to mattress advertisements, they might realize they feel haggard. The attitude toward sleep is shifting. The public is beginning to learn that their sleep needs are biological. There's no shortcut.

Professional sports teams have hired sleep coaches, and athletes are celebrating the performance benefits of sleep. Arianna Huffington wrote an entire book about how she collapsed from lack of sleep and is now on a mission to make people understand how dangerous ignoring sleep needs can be.

We're exposed to more data about our sleep through smartphones and fitness trackers. Hell, we're tired of being tired and aren't willing to take it anymore.

The growing appreciation for sleep and the products that have an impact on it is good for the mattress industry—especially if we continue connecting the mattress to better sleep and keep the public from believing a bottle of pills is the only way to find restorative rest.

An amazing mattress that fits your body gives you much more than a bottle of pills. A more positive attitude, weight loss, better focus throughout the day, improved memory, better sex life, reduction in illness, and a more beautiful appearance are all by-products of a healthy sleep life. How many products in the world can deliver that same list of benefits?

Where Is the Industry Heading?

The landscape for digital disruptors has changed. Tuft & Needle merged with the world's largest bedding manufacturer, Serta Simmons Bedding (SSB). Casper filed for an IPO and took its company public. Since then, Casper's stock has dropped more than 50 percent. It appears investors don't see a clear path to profitability for Casper, which is now true for many direct-to-consumer brands. Purple went public and has experienced success thanks to its great marketing and sleep tech, while Nectar is aggressively expanding into brick and mortar.

Meanwhile, another brand may be a strong predictor of how mattress industry leaders could go about building and managing their brands.

Select Comfort (now Sleep Number) seems to have written a playbook for how direct-to-consumer brands may be built in the future. Sleep Number operates approximately six hundred stores and its annual sales surpass $1 billion. The adjustable air mattress company owns its manufacturing, distribution, and retail operation, and has led the way toward integrating biometric measurement technology into its products, a project we helped with in its early stages. This is a true D2C company that combines online and physical retail to create an end-to-end customer experience that outpaces the market. There's only one other brand that seems to be positioned as well as or better than Sleep Number.

Tempur-Pedic's Preference

No conversation about the state of the mattress industry is complete without talking about Tempur-Pedic. Like Sleep Number, Tempur-Pedic started out telling its story using long-form infomercial advertising. Tempur-Pedic's message was incredibly convincing, and its customer base was happy with the product. This led to Tempur-Pedic becoming the "most recommended brand" in the mattress industry.

Tempur-Pedic is part of Tempur Sealy International (TSI), the result of a merger that combined two of the biggest brands in bedding. After combining with Sealy, Tempur-Pedic experienced a fallout in 2017 with retailer Mattress Firm, the largest bedding chain in the country. Tempur-Pedic continued to thrive even after losing the Mattress Firm business, which accounted for 21 percent of its sales.

TSI then went on a warpath to reengage independent retailers and open more than 200 company-owned Tempur-Pedic stores. The company set this trajectory into motion in the fall of 2015, when Scott Thompson joined TSI as CEO and set out to ensure the company was consumer-centric. The internet had put the consumer in the driver's seat and TSI knew a major shift toward consumer empowerment was taking place. With a firm focus on the shopper, TSI positioned itself to straddle the line between direct-to-consumer sales and brick-and-mortar retail. This balance is the future for most brands.

Scammy Spammy Review Sites

Go to Google and type in "best mattress 2020." A large percentage of first-page results are from spammy review sites. The groups behind these sites are experts at search engine optimization (SEO). They know how to manipulate their websites to ensure Google's algorithm promotes their pages to the top of search results.

When a shopper visits one of these sites, they'll see a variety of reviews, videos, and other content explaining which mattress they should purchase. When the user clicks on the review site's link, they're taken to a mattress website, such as Casper.com—that link is embedded with tracking. If the shopper purchases from the mattress website, that company sends a kickback payment to the spammy review site. This practice is prevalent and not likely to go away without industry action.

Why is this so bad?

Because these spammy sites are incentivized to show the mattress brands that are paying the most money. Many of them are not offering objective advice. Plus, how can review sites truly offer the best product without knowing you, understanding your body shape, preferences, and health issues? The recommendations most mattress sites make are based on little, if any, science, personalization, or testing.

For example, some review sites serve up the "Top 10 Beds for Side Sleepers." Truth is, every human is built differently and has their own set of health considerations, which makes it incredibly hard to say which bed is best. Pressure points, the type of pillow, and a variety of other inputs all impact the feel of a bed. Only after evaluating these critical factors should anyone suggest a bed for a particular customer.

Unfortunately, people searching for mattresses online don't know they're being manipulated by hucksters. The first three pages of Google are flooded with scammy mattress sites, so people never discover the good actors. It's like a bunch of dingy mattress resellers opening hundreds of stores around a clean and well-respected brick-and-mortar retailer. That flood of bad actors makes it impossible for the good store to compete. If shoppers can't find your brand, you don't exist. Spammy review sites own the real estate in Google, create more confusion around a product that is already difficult to shop for, and add no value to the shopper.

Unfortunately, people shopping for a mattress want so badly to be told what to do that they'll listen to anyone that *appears* credible.

Blurred Lines

As online selling began picking up steam, foam suppliers started making mattresses for brands like Casper and other startups. Up until this point, component suppliers who made foam, springs, and fabric primarily sold to mattress manufacturers like Serta, Englander, and Sherwood Bedding.

Today, it's messy. Suppliers sell to consumers and retailers. Traditional manufacturers sell to consumers and retailers. Retailers sell to consumers. Consumers can buy from anyone. It's chaos.

Everyone competes with everyone and there are no clean lines.

Going from Here

That's the lay of the land.

Direct-to-consumer brands disrupted the industry, the majority of people still want to try before buying, several big brands continue to thrive, competition abounds, and review sites are sabotaging the search process.

For brick-and-mortar retailers looking for ways to stand out and attract store traffic, these business conditions might seem impossible to navigate. How do you compete when it's hard for people to find you online?

We have answers.

There are thousands of retailers competing and thriving. We've been on a mission to collect their proven traffic drivers and create a giant list of fun and engaging ideas. As you read this book, we'll take you on a journey to understand why being different matters and how to connect with people, develop an identity that stands out, and make all of this work together.

On top of that, you'll have a list of traffic-driving ideas. When you get stuck, pull out this book, scan through the ideas, and get the creative juices flowing.

Are you ready? Let's get started by getting unstuck.

Chapter Two
Stuck

E arly on a Saturday morning in 2009, I found myself sitting in Leggett & Platt's executive conference room for an "emergency meeting." The CEO, David Haffner, was there along with our COO, Karl Glassman; my boss, Perry Davis, who was the EVP of the Home Furnishings Segment; and Senior Vice President and General Council, Scott Douglas.

Why would we all be together on a Saturday? Was our stock tanking and the executive team gathered to strategize preventing a deeper slide? Nope. We were there because, for some, *change* is a four-letter word. It costs money, brings uncertainty, causes chaos—and is uncomfortable.

Some dumbass (that's me, Mark Quinn) had created a marketing video series that several vocal employees found highly offensive. When it went live, the corporate office was buzzing with opinions. Those opinions snowballed into anger. A small orchestra of people began calling for my job. They wanted me fired. Dave Haffner called the meeting to discuss what to do about the uproar.

Employees were angry because the video series clashed with their view of Leggett & Platt as a 126-year-old company built by wire-benders and blacksmiths. The culture was made up of small-town, hardworking people. When the marketing group produced a video featuring two dudes in a bar talking about getting laid, there was a backlash.

Even though most workers were very humble, in actuality, Leggett & Platt was a behemoth in the bedding business. The company is the world's largest producer of innersprings for the mattress industry, making components that improve people's sleep and quality of life.

Leggett never really wanted to be out front. We were happy letting our customers, the bedding producers, lead the way. But when I came on board, the innerspring industry was facing significant challenges. Chinese spring makers were subsidizing their innerspring factories and selling goods into the United States below our cost to produce (that's called *dumping*).

We were losing market share and closing factories.

I felt it was time for Leggett & Platt to position itself not just as wire-benders but as thought leaders in the mattress industry. When competitors are beating you up on price every day, you have to get creative. It was time for us to step up and step out.

My team and our marketing agency, owned by Brent Beshore and led by Emily Holdman, decided to produce a web series for Leggett & Platt called *The Virgin Mattress*.

The goal was to increase the frequency of mattress purchases by getting people to understand that taking a "hand-me-down" mattress wasn't a good idea. It's not uncommon for parents to pass along their old mattress to a young couple getting married.

Do you want to sleep on the same mattress your parents had sex on?

All together now...GROSS!

Beyond sex, beds become disgusting over time. You drool and sweat when you sleep. If you take someone's old mattress, you're probably sleeping in their drool and sweat, not to mention tiny little corpses of dust mites and who knows what else.

We decided to tell people, "Don't sleep on that hand-me-down. You are better off getting a fresh *virgin* mattress." We called the web video series *The Virgin Mattress*, and episode 1 opens with two college buddies sitting at their favorite bar, drinking beer.

Tom: Hey man, congratulations on the engagement; you and Vanessa are going to make a great couple.

Rusty: Thanks, I really love her and I think this is a good thing for us.

Tom: So how is the big move going? Is she letting you keep any of your furniture from the fraternity house?

Rusty: Are you kidding!? She got rid of everything, including the velvet Elvis paintings, but I am getting to keep my bed.

Tom: Seriously? Dude, that bed has a lot of history. Even I got laid on that mattress.

As you read that dialogue, you might be thinking it's not any worse than what's on television today. You'd be correct. But that didn't matter. Culture is what mattered. And we injected

The Virgin Mattress video series directly into a culture we didn't fully understand.

Instead of testing the video concept on a small group of Leggett employees, we emailed all nineteen thousand employees across the globe for the big launch. "Please watch this and share it with your friends and family," we asked.

They watched it alright. Many watched it with daggers shooting from their eyeballs. Thankfully, the executive team at Leggett rallied together and took ownership of the mistake and we pushed on.

For me, *The Virgin Mattress* was a major public fail.

Failing sucks. It's embarrassing and costly, and can damage your reputation. Failure can get in your head and plant seeds of self-doubt that may impact your decision-making.

You are going to fail if you're pushing hard enough. That is a fact of life. The important thing to consider is how you let failure impact your business.

Will failure beat you down and prevent you from trying the next thing? Or will you get back on the proverbial horse, smack its ass, and ride to the finish?

Failure is one reason people resist change.

You're running your business and spinning plates as fast as you can, trying not to let any crash to the floor. Before you know it, things aren't going as well. Hiring people is a major problem because the workforce has changed, the delivery staff are hard to keep around, and e-commerce sellers have gobbled up 20 to 30 percent of the market share in your industry. To make things worse, store traffic ain't what it used to be, even though you keep increasing budgets.

Sure, you're looking for answers, but you're not making any big moves. Why? Because change is complicated and often involves factors like legacy, status quo, hubris, and comfort zones.

Legacy: Maybe you own a multigenerational business and Dad still has the reins and looks at things through the lens of what built the company. Even though what worked before doesn't work anymore.

Status quo: Maybe you're okay with the current results and happy to go with the status quo. What happens when that approach doesn't work anymore? Lack of initiative causes you to crash into a wall you never saw coming because you weren't paying attention.

There's also the issue of the "whack-a-mole boss." Anytime this leader is in a meeting and a fresh idea pops up, he gets out a big rubber mallet and crushes it as fast as he can. At some point, the rest of the moles say "screw this" and stop poking their head up, because they know what's coming.

Ever meet Mr. We've Tried That?

You: Hey boss, why don't we try selling beds by talking about the benefits of sleep, instead of just pushing price and promotion?

Mr. We've Tried That: Jimmy from the ad department ran a spot like that in 1974 and it really didn't work.

You: Isn't it possible that Jimmy wrote shitty copy and that's why the ad failed?

Mr. We've Tried That: You're fired for talking about my cousin Jimmy.

My least favorite are the arrogant leaders who don't like any idea that's not their own.

Comfort zone: You are never standing still; you are always in motion. I remember a conference where a guy burst onto the stage riding a unicycle. Eventually he paused, rocking back and forth to keep himself from falling over. Then he made his point: "Life is just like trying to ride this unicycle. You are never standing still. You are either moving backwards or moving forwards, just like I am now."

Minor tweaks are useful when it comes to refining a process. But every now and then you have to blow stuff up.

Montgomery Ward, Levitz Furniture, Blockbuster, Radio Shack, Toys"R"Us, Sharper Image—take your pick—these companies didn't think change was necessary, pivoted too late, or tried the wrong strategy at the wrong time and failed. They lived in their comfort zone for so long they died in it.

Comfort is the enemy of innovation and progress. At some point, you have to rip the binkie out of your mouth and charge into the unknown. That is where the real magic happens.

Too many retailers live off the crack cocaine of product, price, and promotion advertising. Why? Because they think these things matter most to consumers. They're wrong! If you really want to bring consumers back into your stores, you must look at opportunities in a new way. Push past what's comfortable and go after what's possible.

Case in Point...

Back to *The Virgin Mattress* debacle. We scrapped all seven episodes and remade the entire series in a kinder, gentler way.

It was only a moderate success, primarily because it wasn't bold enough. But even though the revised *Virgin Mattress* didn't pack the punch I wanted, it led to something bigger.

By this time, Leggett & Platt was facing another business

threat. Innersprings were losing market share to specialty foam suppliers.

A few mattress brands had spent hundreds of millions of dollars to convince consumers that innersprings were old technology and foam and air beds were better. The erosion of market share was beginning to hurt Leggett's business, so we had to figure out a way to reverse that trend. Innersprings needed to be "the cool kid" again.

I remember sitting around a conference table at Leggett's corporate headquarters in Carthage, Missouri, and Mark Kinsley asking me, "What's the conversation around innersprings?" I told him the narrative with the most traction was "springs suck and foam's great."

Kinsley said we had to change the conversation: "The worst comeback when someone says you suck is 'No I don't; *you* suck.' People are convinced springs are squeaky old technology. We can't try to say we're better. We have to change the conversation."

I remember watching a golf tournament on Sunday morning and seeing a great commercial about hybrid golf clubs. Another ad celebrated the newest hybrid car. At that moment I heard a gong go off in my brain. I jumped up and started making notes.

For years, mattresses had been made with both springs and foam. It wasn't an either/or proposition. Together springs and foam were better. Together they were a hybrid. That language was familiar to consumers, and we thought people would understand it.

Before we launched another video series, we asked retail sales associates (RSAs) to use the term "hybrid mattress" in the selling process and tell us their observations. The RSAs reported back that people understood the term, it increased their average ticket, and from door-to-desk it shortened the sales cycle.

Our team also did an internet sweep and discovered that nobody was using the term "hybrid" to define a mattress. A search audit showed FurnitureToday.com had never used it. This left things wide open for us to define hybrid mattresses in a way that served Leggett & Platt.

We created our own category. The language freshened things up and gave bedding producers and retailers a new way to talk about the latest sleep technology. And we positioned Leggett & Platt's Comfort Core innersprings among the heroes of the story.

The RSAs liked hybrids and consumers understood the term, so we knew we were onto something. The question was, how do we get an entire industry to adopt our new way of thinking? Naturally, we decided to make a rap video.

Through a partnership with Second City Communications out of Chicago, we created a rap video about hybrid mattresses called "Get Hybrid." Go to YouTube and search for "Get Hybrid Mattress Rap"; it's worth the two minutes and fifty-six seconds, I swear. We think you'll agree that it is, without a doubt, the best mattress rap video ever produced.

Provided by Leggett & Platt

That "Get Hybrid" video was like a Super Bowl commercial. It was a large part of a broader strategy to push major mattress manufacturers into using the term "hybrid." One year after the campaign launched, Sealy aired a national television ad with a product called the Sealy Hybrid, becoming the first major to embrace the new category and validating our strategy.

The hybrid mattress was eventually adopted by every major bedding producer, including some of the companies that had been attacking springs for years. Hybrids soon became the fastest-growing and most profitable segment in the industry.

The results were measurable. We had reversed the erosion. Leggett was no longer losing market share, and innersprings outpaced specialty foams for nine out of the next ten quarters, generating millions in sales and profits.

The executive team at Leggett & Platt could have fired me because of the disruption around *The Virgin Mattress*, but they didn't. Instead, they stood by me and had the courage to push even harder—to evolve as a company and protect their core business.

Imagine me going to Leggett's leadership after the *Virgin Mattress* debacle and asking them to fund a six-figure rap music video about a hybrid mattress—a category that didn't even exist. They said yes, and it paid off big. Our business shot up by over 30 percent, bringing millions in profit to the company and to our customers, the bedding producers that jumped on the hybrid train.

You will fail. But if, over time, you stay true to your strategy, you will succeed.

If you want to ignore your problems, there are 1,001 ways to justify inaction, but we know where that leads. Be bold. Take action.

Are you ready to get *unstuck*? It all starts with a simple decision, and it's yours to make.

(That's enough from Quinn for now. In the next chapter, we're back to the collective wisdom of Dos Marcos!)

Chapter Three

Decide to Do It Differently

D r. Dre said there are three types of people (we're paraphrasing): Those who know what's going on. Those who don't. And people like us that make shit happen.

If you're going to change the course of business and life, you must make a decision to stop repeating the past. When you look up and realize the internet has forever altered the way you gain customers, you must change your approach. Quit doing what's safe. Step out and take that leap of faith.

Decide to do it differently.

Why Being Different Matters

We live in an attention economy. If you capture people's attention, you get paid. Fail to make people look and listen, and business will suffer. Offer the same products sold at a dirty-window store down the road, and you'll be commoditized. Avoid building value in your products, and no one will care what you're selling. Promote only price and item, and someone will beat your price. You need to differentiate.

Being different matters for two main reasons.

Normal and mundane gets ignored. If you don't grab people's attention, they won't listen to anything you have to say. Maybe you want to tell people how a high-quality mattress can deliver better sleep and change their lives. You want to talk about your sixty-two-year-old family-run business and why it should matter to shoppers. You want consumers to know about same-day delivery, financing options, and your friendly people. No one will listen to any of that unless you first grab their attention. And to do that, you have to be different.

A unique brand deepens your connection to people and insulates your company from competition. Rick Anderson is the former President of Tempur-Pedic North America. In September of 2019, Anderson was a guest on the *Dos Marcos* mattress podcast and cited a staggering statistic: strip away all of its assets and the Tempur-Pedic brand is valued at $3.5 billion. That's just the brand!

A strong brand creates a moat around your business. The store down the street can always beat you at something. They can peddle knockoff products. They can undercut your prices. But brands are nearly impossible to knock off. And when built properly, brands create trust. "Any damn fool can put on a deal," the ad tycoon David Ogilvy once said, "but it takes genius, faith, and perseverance to create a brand."

How does a retailer create a brand that people prefer, trust, and look to first when they enter the shopping phase? You'll find our answers later in the book. The first step is simple: decide to do it differently.

The Mattress World Changed

Many old mattress dogs feel like they woke up in a world they don't understand. How could a group of internet nerds who don't know a lick about the bedding business swoop in and sell more mattresses on a website than many large chains sell in stores?

While the mattress industry continued selling through the traditional value chain of component supplier, manufacturer, retailer, then consumer, a group of hip, young gunslingers looked at our industry and decided to do it differently.

If your business is thriving, odds are you made a decision to forge a fresh path through the jungle. But if it feels like disruption is destroying your business, you need to rethink your entire approach. It's time to cut through the clutter with fresh thinking, innovative business models, and your finger on the pulse of what makes business move in the new economy.

To generate foot traffic and sales, you have to give people a compelling reason to put on pants and stop shopping at Amazon.com.

You have to decide to do it differently.

Consciousness of Current Choices

When making a new decision, you first need to become conscious of current choices.

Right now you're choosing your mindset. You're selecting where to put your time. You're choosing to do what used to work. You and your business are a result of your choices. There's nobody else to blame.

At this moment, you've chosen to operate your business the way it's operating. You've chosen to live in your house. You've chosen to drive a certain vehicle. That car may not be your first choice, but you did choose it. You and only you are responsible for the decisions you make.

Odds are, leading up to this point, nobody forced you to do anything. You need to accept responsibility for every single thing that's happened thus far. And if something happened that was completely out of your control, forgive and move on.

Before you can make meaningful change, you must come to grips with this fact. You get to decide. Once you decide, you must own your choice.

If you don't like the previous choices you've made, rethink the path forward. Make new choices. Put new plans in place. Reimagine your future.

Decide to do it differently.

Why Different Works

The human brain is wired to ignore almost everything mundane. Everyday events get processed like canned goods on a grocery clerk's conveyor belt. But the moment something surprises our brains, we stop and pay attention.

If the grocery checker suddenly pulled a poodle across the scanner, he would pause with surprise.

Surprises grab attention. The majority of events unfolding on a given day are too predictable to command your attention. Things like driving to work on the same route or eating at the same restaurant are part of the schema that's familiar to your brain. But when there's a high-speed police chase zooming along your route to work, your brain gets jolted from its pattern recognition. That high-speed chase violates the schema.

When a person sees something truly surprising, her eyebrows curve upward, her eyes open wider, and her jaw drops. The mouth opens, yet not to speak. In their book *Made to Stick*, authors Dan and Chip Heath say, "It's as though our bodies want to ensure that we're not talking or moving when we ought to be taking in new information." When we're surprised, we start asking, "What's going on?"

According to the Heath brothers, surprise gets our attention and interest keeps our attention.

In most situations, our brains are on autopilot. Walk to the fridge, grab the jelly, spread on bread, blah, blah, blah. Our brains are constantly guessing what's next, and they're really good at making predictions.

When something comes along that interrupts that schema, our senses focus and our attention jerks toward the new element. If you're spreading jelly on the bread and a bird bashes into the plate glass window, you're going to look. And if that bird is colored like a rainbow, you're going to inspect it.

You inspect the bird because the crash startled you. It was scary. As your mind registered there was no real threat, a mystery began playing in your head. What is a rainbow-colored bird doing in this part of the country? What kind of bird is it? Mysteries are open loops. Brains hate open loops. We want to close those loops. Open loops mean the outcome is unknown. If the outcome is unknown, it could be either threatening or desirable.

David Ogilvy placed an eye patch on the man in the Hathaway shirt and catapulted his client's business.

Trent Ranburger dressed up as both Dr. Evil and Austin Powers and created a commercial for his mattress store. The spot ended up on national television and was ranked sixth on a list of the world's dumbest commercials. Trent Bedding has been the top-rated mattress store in Bowling Green, Kentucky, for ten years straight, and he's a local celebrity people seek out to help with their sleep needs.

Jesse Cole wears a yellow tuxedo and named his baseball team the Savannah Bananas. They have a break-dancing first base coach, grandma beauty pageants, and a parking lot penguin to guide traffic. Season tickets are impossible to get, and every game is a sellout.

Our brains are designed to pay attention to what's different. Decide to do it differently, and you can win.

Deciding to Do It Differently

There are three separate action items embedded in the sentence "Decide to do it differently."

You must make a **conscious choice** that you're going to **take action** in **novel ways**.

To repeat: you CAN do it!

- Choice
- Action
- Novelty

You're making up your mind in advance. You're committing to taking action. Your actions will be unlike what you've done in the past.

You'll Be Criticized

Those who act differently will be criticized. Be prepared. Those who stand out earn reactions and feedback. Some will be negative, some positive.

The worst outcome is getting no reaction. The middle is death; silence means you're being ignored. Remember, emotion drives action and action drives sales. Get people fired up. Get them to feel something, and the reaction you create will benefit your business.

Breakthrough ideas will attract love and hate reactions. You'll often hear the negative before the positive, so be prepared. Grow thick skin. Listen to all the feedback, but don't let it get to you.

The boldest and biggest in business commit to their plans. Don't fold at the first sign of adversity. One attempt at being different will make little difference. Consistency over time will produce results. Know what you're committing to and do the work.

It will take tenacity. You'll be the comedian on stage dodging tomatoes. Keep telling your jokes and soon you'll start seeing smiles. Then you'll hear laughter. And one day you'll look up at a room full of people who paid to hear your jokes.

Showing You're Different

Once you've decided to be different, you must take action to show how unique you are.

In 1874, John Robinson was looking for a way to prove that the newly completed Eads Bridge was sturdy. The circus was in St. Louis that week and Robinson found an elephant to walk across the bridge spanning the Mississippi River.

At that time, elephants were believed to have an innate sense of danger. The public believed the beast wouldn't walk across the bridge if it was weak. Surrounded by the sound of cheering crowds, the elephant completed the walk across the bridge. Robinson then sent locomotives chugging over the bridge to prove to people the bridge was safe.

In doing this, Robinson took a novel approach to proving the bridge was sound. Quoting statistics about architecture and engineering wouldn't have worked, because fear is an emotion. People were scared of the bridge because it was made with arches that looked different. The waters of the Mississippi were flowing fast beneath.

The public needed something symbolic and visible they could trust. Robinson's elephant walk instilled confidence in a way that was unique, memorable, and impossible to ignore.

Authentic and Different

Unless you happen to have an elephant lying around, discovering your own unique, memorable, and impossible-to-ignore qualities might be a challenge. So, what does being different look like for *you*? What if you're sort of normal? What if you love numbers and don't consider yourself creative?

Wacky can work. But only if you're wacky. What if you're more of a wonk than a wack? More scholar than clown?

Being different isn't reserved for zany people. You need to uncover *your* brand of different and apply it to your business.

A shift takes place when you decide to do it differently. Suddenly you go from playing basketball against giants to running sprints against sloths. No one can keep up. They don't understand what you're doing or why you're doing it. They scoff and criticize. They sneer and talk trash. And then one day, you see those trash-talkers trying to play your game.

At first you'll be upset. Don't worry. If someone else plays your game, they won't be as good at it as you are. It won't take long before your competitor realizes they're the sloth and you're the track star.

A key piece of your game will be something fun, meaningful, and magical: connecting with people. That's where we're heading next.

Chapter Four

Connecting

In early 2020, we experienced something unexpected and unprecedented in the coronavirus outbreak. We Zoomed and FaceTimed with friends and family, but most of us couldn't be in the presence of our friends, neighbors, or coworkers.

This separation eventually took its toll, even for introverts. Remember those famous images of Italians standing out on their balconies, singing and dancing?

We need to feel connected to others. Humans are social beings. Building a strong bond with others is a superpower that can change just about everything in business and life. If you have strong connections to your family, your friends, your employees, and consumers in your market, your business should thrive. If those relationships aren't there, you will always fall short of the opportunity to make an impact.

In order to attract foot traffic and make people fall in love with your store, you need consumers to know more than what your business sells. They also need to know who you are and why you're in business. Here's how Mike Whitaker of Nationwide Marketing puts it: "You need to answer three key questions. Who are we? What do we do? What do we believe?" Connecting is a must if you want to reach rock-star status. *New York Times* bestselling author Roy H. Williams recently said that "People don't bond to companies. They bond to personalities."

Are you running a retail store that simply offers consumers a place to buy stuff? Or have you built a business that has become the preferred place to shop in your community? One is purely transactional. The other has the potential to capture hearts and minds, drive sales, and deliver higher margins.

Jim "Mattress Mack" McIngvale from Gallery Furniture in Houston, Texas, is a case study on how to do it differently. He is also a great example of someone who understands how to meaningfully connect with people.

During Hurricane Harvey, Jim opened two of his stores and welcomed over four hundred people from the Houston area who were displaced after flooding swallowed their homes. A reporter asked Jim why he was turning stores into shelters. "Being together in a space is helpful for all of us," McIngvale told *Time*. "People don't feel like they're on their own."

Jim understood what people were feeling and needing and how to calm their fears. As a result, he has since created raving fans and a deep bond with people in Houston who prefer to buy bedding and furniture at Gallery Furniture.

Look to Your Roots

When it comes to figuring out how to connect with your community, no group offers more advice and supports more furniture and mattress retailers than Nationwide Marketing Group.

Nationwide is the leading marketing and operational support organization for more than five thousand independent retailers in the rent-to-own space, custom installers in major appliances, consumer electronics, furniture, mattresses, home theater, and the outdoor industries.

Dos Marcos has been the headline speaker at their national events, and we regularly teach classes during their learning sessions. We get to meet store owners and staff, hear about their companies, and help them figure out how to take their businesses to the next level.

These retailers tell us stories about how Grandad started the company or about their first job unloading trucks in the warehouse. They recount tales of raising money for local charities, serving on boards, and supporting local baseball and softball teams. We love hearing how they build community and connection because we're convinced those stories matter to consumers.

But often, when you go to these retailers' websites and click on the "About Us" pages, it looks like someone copied and pasted generic marketing text. "We are a family-run business committed to helping people find high-quality furniture at affordable prices." That statement is boring and wildly underdeveloped.

Big-box stores and online retailers can kick your ass when it comes to low prices, better financing offers, exclusive products, and expanded assortments. But they can't come close to your ability to connect with the people in your town.

Their grandparents didn't live in the same neighborhood as your grandparents. Their kids don't attend the same schools as your kids. You never see them at Friday night football games and their name is rarely (if ever) on the front of the local soccer team's jersey. You have the winning hand. You just have to play it.

There are three simple rules when it comes to building trust and forging a bond with your community.

Be authentic: Authenticity is about aligning with who you really are. Don't sponsor the baseball team just because you think it's a good way to get your name out there. Sponsor the team because you care about the kids in your town and you want to give them a chance to play sports.

Know your brand. If riding an elephant around your car lot screaming "Sale!" isn't your thing, don't do it. Tell your story and promote your business in your voice. Fly your flag and you will find your fans.

Be intentional about telling your story: Humility is an excellent quality. There seems to be too little of it. But when it comes to sharing who you are and why you exist, blow your horn and blow it loudly! For some, that's not easy. Maybe you're not a bragger, or you don't think your story matters. Stay with us and we'll provide a roadmap on how to do this in a way that serves you and your customers.

Conduct Your Business with Integrity: Trust is the cornerstone of any strong relationship and you can't have trust if you play games with your pricing, if you mislead people in your advertising, or if you hard-close customers to get the deal. Are you playing the long game or just trying to get the deal in front of you? Do you want to *sell* the person in your store or do you want to *serve* them, their friends, and their relatives for the next fifty years? If you earn people's trust, you have a significant advantage over your competitors.

Consumers make buying decisions based on emotion, not logic. If they genuinely like your company, you have a shot at getting them into your store when the time comes to buy what you're selling. If people *love* your company, you're even more likely to get their business.

When you take your car to a mechanic and they fix the problem without charging you because it was a minor issue, do you trust them, tell your friends about them, and go back to them? Do you even consider a different mechanic the next time your car is making "that noise"? How do you *feel* when you frequent that little restaurant in your town where the owner flutters by your table to say hello and ask about your family? Would you even consider going somewhere else to celebrate your wedding anniversary?

It all comes down to purpose.

If you are in business to sell stuff and make a profit, you can be successful on some level. If, on the other hand, you are in business to help people solve their problems, then you are playing a different game than most of your competitors—a game you will win because you are invested in connecting.

So what's the best way to build this connection to people?

Capture Foot Traffic with a CAGE

If you want foot traffic, you need a CAGE.

We know what you're thinking: great, another business book with an acronym that promises to solve all my problems. (Spoiler alert: there are more to come!) But the principles of CAGE really work, so give it a chance.

CAGE is a simple way to remember where to put your focus as you work to drive foot traffic and authentically connect with people. It stands for:

- Community
- Answers
- Giving
- Experiences

As you carve out a unique position in your marketplace, we recommend treating your approach like a major in college. For example, you may earn a degree in *giving* with a minor in *answers*. By focusing on one or two principles within CAGE, you'll strengthen your reputation and deepen your brand awareness.

As you read this next section, consider your strengths and pay close attention to the examples of *how* retailers make the CAGE strategies come to life. We will dive even deeper into how to trumpet your story in chapter 8, so take some notes and start thinking about how to apply this framework to your own business.

Community

During the spring of 2020, as the coronavirus crippled the economy, small businesses shut down. Mattress stores closed up shop. But while the pandemic crushed communities across the country, retailers like Trent Bedding were there for people in their hometowns.

As we mentioned earlier, Trent Bedding is owned and operated by Trent Ranburger. The people of Bowling Green, Kentucky, have voted Trent Bedding the top mattress store for ten years running.

When the coronavirus started spreading sickness and fear, Trent committed to keeping a positive spirit. Trent is known for his funny television commercials and his presence on social media. So he posted a funny picture or video every day, spreading joy while staying "on brand."

As the gravity of the economic situation continued to weigh, Trent took his community involvement a step further by posting on social media about Bowling Green–based businesses people could continue to support. Trent called it the

Local Business Challenge. One post read, "You can help local businesses during this time by simply liking their page and giving them a follow! Today's businesses are Split Tree Barbeque, Curbside Ministries, Look Sharp Dry Cleaners, Geno's Italian Deli, Comfort Keepers In-Home Senior Care."

Even though people were hunkered down and practicing social distancing, Trent knew they were active on social media and treated this as an opportunity to serve fellow small-business owners by helping them build their social followings. He focused on community, the "C" in CAGE.

How are you involved in your community? Do you sit on any boards? Are you part of Rotary? Do you support youth sports or belong to any organizations? If you are actively involved in the community, use social channels, press releases, advertising, and blog posts to talk about what's going on.

If you have a passion for community but aren't actively engaged, it's time to get involved. No more sitting on the sidelines.

You can also look at the people working for your business. Which parts of the community are they serving? Use your platform to talk about what they're doing. It gives you a chance to shine a light on your people, focus on their contributions, and bring attention to the groups they are working with.

If you're in the sleep business, have you ever considered giving free talks about the benefits of sleep? What if you went to the senior center and talked about how to get better sleep as you get older? Maybe do something fun for grade school kids to educate them on why they need to stop drinking so much caffeine! Who is really teaching kids about sleep? It's not the schools. Maybe this is a cause you could champion.

If public speaking isn't your thing, find someone on your staff who is capable. Maybe you can produce sleep education content for your blog or Facebook page. And if you go down the path of serving your community with information, you might find that providing answers is the most invigorating piece of the CAGE.

Answers

Jeff Scheuer owns a bedding store called Mattress to Go in Shelby Township, Michigan. From that store, Jeff produces his Beducation YouTube channel. The videos have earned more than 1.5 million views and helped thousands of people navigate the confusion that comes with buying a mattress. Jeff was also a coach for the 1994 US Olympic luge team. During those games, Gordy Sheer became the first American to earn a medal in luge. Jeff has a passion for coaching and bringing out the best in others—whether he's mentoring athletes or helping people buy the best mattress for their needs.

The "A" in CAGE stands for Answers. Jeff is a shining example of someone who used his passion for coaching to turn himself into a one-man answers department.

During the shopping phase consumers are looking for answers. They're confused. When they find a trustworthy guide to assist with bed buying, they feel like Luke Skywalker discovering Yoda in the swamp. "Finally, someone to show me the Force is with me ... and to explain all this talk about springs and foam."

Jeff noticed that people shopping in his stores didn't know the first thing about buying a bed. That's because the industry has made it so confusing. The same beds have different names at different stores. There's significant price elasticity with so many promotions that you never know if you are getting a good deal. Then you stir in the review sites full of people pretending to know what they're talking about, and things become a hot mess, fast.

Jeff created a brand around Beducation and began producing videos addressing every customer question he could think of.

"Don't Buy a Mattress Based upon Warranty" has more than eight thousand views. "The truth about 50% off mattress sales" has nearly 160,000 views. Jeff's top-ranked video has a title that does not tantalize: "Polyurethane foam, memory foam and latex foam." That video has attracted more than 250,000 views.

Jeff is helping his audience while adding value to their shopping process. Of course he wants to sell products, but for him the videos are about serving people and giving them a resource. The Beducator helps shoppers understand the importance of better sleep and guides them through the frustrating process of buying a new bed.

If you came across someone who offered useful information and education, would you buy from them? If you understood that person was more about *helping you* than *selling you*, would it impact your decision about where to buy? Would you go on to tell your friends about him?

Look for ways to give your customers valuable information. Make their lives easier by pushing the sale aside. By providing answers, you build trust and make your store the preferred place to shop.

You will gain friends and customers for life.

Be the answer. Deliver the information. Help people navigate a nebulous buying process, and they will reward you with their business.

Giving

Michael Grossman is a fourth-generation furniture man who owns Kensington Furniture in Northfield, New Jersey. Northfield is a town near Atlantic City where casino money has long powered the local economy.

The Atlantic City area has faced some of the worst economic downturns in the nation. Back in 2016, four casinos closed their doors within ninety days, wiping out thousands of jobs. Those displaced workers were thousands of potential customers for Kensington Furniture and other small businesses.

Having been around since 1912, Kensington Furniture has faced many difficult times and continues finding ways to prosper and to give back to a community in need.

When workers around Northfield found themselves out of a job, Grossman and his team realized that life continued for their children. Soccer games went on. The marching band marched. And prom night was still expected to be a magical affair, with all the girls gowned up in dazzling dresses.

Kensington Furniture isn't in the clothing business, but that didn't stop Michael and his team from filling the store with beautiful dresses and giving them away to those in need. Since then, Project Prom has become an annual volunteer event to collect and distribute prom dresses and accessories for less fortunate high school students.

Community members drop off new or gently worn gowns at Kensington Furniture. Once the store has enough dresses to meet the anticipated demand, young people from all over the area make a trip to Kensington Furniture, where the showroom has been transformed with fitting rooms and racks of dresses in different colors and sizes.

Instead of spending prom night in a gown that's uncomfortable or old, each young lady walks away with a beautiful dress. On prom night they get to wear something that helps them feel confident and beautiful. All thanks to the giving spirit of the people at Kensington Furniture.

Giving feels good. And it can be good for businesses looking for a way to bring traffic to their store. In the case of Kensington Furniture, the first wave of people visiting the store were all dropping off prom dresses. The second group of people were parents and children picking up prom dresses. Neither stream of foot traffic would have happened if Kensington Furniture hadn't been giving back.

To show your heart and passion for helping, you can give money, time, talent, and products. You can give space to those who need to hold an event. The options for giving are nearly endless. And the opinions around how to give are wide-ranging.

In the furniture and mattress business, many companies are led by people with big hearts. Often these people are influenced by their faiths. They want to give from the goodness of those large hearts, but they are reluctant to tell anyone about it because, as scripture says, "when you give to the needy, do not let your left hand know what the right hand is doing" (Matthew 6:1–4). This approach is understandable, but consider placing the focus on the charity instead of yourself, and see what happens.

What if your giving inspired others to do the same? When your gifts become public, does that attract customers who share your values? Many consumers are searching for companies they agree with. They prefer to patronize businesses that share their values and reflect their hearts.

When faced with two options—celebrate your giving or keep it private—choose both.

Keep some of your giving private, while making other parts known to the public. This allows you to fulfill your desire to give in private, while still inspiring your community, connecting with your employees, and giving people a glimpse into the heart of your business.

People want to do business with those they know and like. People like companies that reflect what's in their souls.

If you are going to make *giving* a central part of your company's identity, keep in mind the things that can go wrong. Sometimes giving can do more harm than good. People can sniff out a phony. If donating a portion of sales to a charity is just a ploy to sell more products, it will eventually become apparent, and you'll damage your reputation and lose customers' trust.

Even if your heart is in the right place, how you design a program that combines giving with products matters.

When you're talking about your company's efforts to help a charitable organization, make it about them, not you. Resist the urge to fit all of the typical promotional offers into your ad. Instead, shine a light on the benefactor of your efforts.

If you hitch your business to a cause, make sure your purpose is to serve that cause. It's better if you can personalize the effort. If you establish a link between yourself and the charity, your customers will see a deep and authentic connection.

Now that you understand the minefield of giving, let's look at some examples that were authentic and connected a business to a cause.

- **James Reasoner at Mattress World** donated upper-end mattresses to the fire department, who spread the word by snapping pictures and posting to social media with fire trucks in the background.
- **Katy Law with Sweet Dreams** in Lake Norman, North Carolina, said foot traffic increased during an in-store

mattress and furniture fundraiser benefiting local middle schools. They held the event on a Sunday when the store is normally closed.

- **Mitch Roy with International Furniture Wholesale** asked customers to bring in a single nonperishable item to receive 20 percent off anything in the store. Also, Roy and his team did free in-home consultations and room deals where they handled donating all the items to charity for the customer.

- **Mike Bruegge with Bruegge and Co.** offered a discount of 1 percent for each canned good a customer brought into the store (up to twenty-five cans).

- **Tony Howell with Rooms Unlimited** drove more foot traffic and showed the company's heart for helping by offering a 25 percent discount to customers who donated twenty-five dollars to the Susan G. Komen breast cancer foundation.

For a strategy of giving to work, it must be authentic and you must celebrate each gift. If you keep all of your charity quiet, the public will not know your heart. You will forfeit the ability to attract people searching for companies they want to do business with.

Experiences

A lot has changed since the 1940s when Mom went to a store, purchased flour, eggs, milk, and cocoa and mixed it together to make a birthday cake.

In 1947, Betty Crocker came along with cake mixes that combined several commodities and shortened the time it took to make a birthday cake. Then, when baking became too time-consuming, moms and dads began buying their kids pre-made birthday cakes.

You might expect the progression of economic value to stop at buying a fully made item, but there's another layer to this cake.

Today, parents rent out trampoline parks or Chuck E. Cheese, and the cake is included for free—as part of the experience.

We live in the *experience economy*. People would rather pay for experiences than for physical goods. It's why Disney World costs seventeen cents per minute and Starbucks can charge five dollars for a cup of coffee. People love experiences.

Think about how the process of getting a car serviced has evolved. In the old days, you drove to the dealership, dropped off your car, sat in a grungy room that smelled like burnt coffee in a chair held together by duct tape, and watched old episodes of *Let's Make a Deal* on a black-and-white television. Nowadays, you pull your car under a portico and a guy dressed in khaki pants and a nice polo is at your door before you've stopped the car. He opens the door for you, introduces himself, and begins the process of getting your car checked in for its appointment. Then you're escorted into a customer lounge featuring leather sofas and a mini fridge fully stocked with bottled water. If you're in the mood, you can make yourself a nice espresso at the complimentary coffee bar. Don't have time to wait? That's not a problem. The dealership will get you a courtesy car to drive while yours is being fixed, or they will chauffeur you to your gym to get in a workout while you wait.

Shopping online is typically more convenient than shopping in person. But families often want to get out of the house. They want to connect around a shared experience. Shoppers want to see something new and different. They want to be entertained, laugh, and sometimes even cry.

Experiences come in many shapes and sizes. Sometimes they cost money; other times they are free. Sometimes they solve a problem, and other times they simply make someone smile.

Have you been to a running shoe store lately? At most of the nicer running shoe shops, they have a treadmill equipped with cameras. The salesperson asks you to get on the treadmill and jog while the camera captures your gait.

From there, the trained salesperson can identify any issues with how your foot lands on the surface and observe how your body might be compensating for incorrect form.

The salesperson is figuring out which shoes you should try. Do you need extra arch support because your foot folds inward? Perhaps you have a neutral running style and therefore need a neutral shoe—in which case corrective footwear would hurt your form and likely lead to pain.

It seems obvious. Of course you should get fitted for the right shoe. If you are a serious runner, you don't want to develop issues that could become chronic.

In the mattress business, we need to take a similar approach. People need to be fitted for the proper mattress. If someone walks in and asks what's the best mattress, that should lead to a series of questions about aches and pains, sleeping style, whether they sleep with a partner, pets, medical issues, and a variety of other topics. Those questions should lead to a mattress fitting. It should be an enjoyable experience that connects that person to the right mattress for their body and sleeping style.

Another fun in-store experience is what Mark Quinn calls the Princess and the Pea. Place a small stack of cash between the mattress and box spring. Have people go from mattress to mattress, try each one, and identify the bed they think is hiding the money. Those who guess correctly get put into a drawing. At the end of the month, pull one name out of a hat, and that person wins the cash.

This experience gets everyone who enters your store to try all your mattresses. Or you can design it to direct customers to certain mattresses you want them to try because you believe in those products or know that many happy customers have purchased them.

There are many ways to create a great experience:

- **Troy Simmons with Bel Furniture** organized a tailgate party with the local school football team and drill team and held a chili cook-off.

- **Millers Furniture of Lancaster** held a "meet the builder day." Luceeta Rohrer brought in the Amish crafts- men who actually made the furniture. Customers had a chance to visit and engage with the builders while eating Amish cookies and homemade ice cream.

- There's a superhero working at **Sweet Dreams Mattress and Furniture** in Lake Norman, North Carolina. He takes the experience out of the store and brings it to the people. Andrew Schlesser, better known as Matt- man, wears a mattress costume to 5K running events and hosts charity gatherings like the First Responders Support Services Fundraiser. This sleep superhero creates a fun experience for people in the community. It's all part of Mattman's ongoing mission to "fight the things that keep us up at night, so you can fall asleep faster, and stay asleep longer so you can get the good night's sleep that you deserve." The Lake Norman Chamber of Commerce recognized Schlesser with the 2019 John R. Cherry Community Service Award.

- **Laurie Warner with Randolph Home Furnishings** hosted a girls' night out event for ladies in Ohio.

- **Bethany Scanlon with Ocean Breeze Bedding** attracted customers by bringing in a yoga and health instructor for "an evening of creating your best night of sleep." They held a drawing for a free yoga-and-wellness bundle.

- **Dustin Schmidt of Schmidt's America's Mattress** store partnered with a local radio station for a My Mattress Sucks contest and had people post pictures of their mattress to the store's Facebook page.

- **Orsini's in Martinsburg, West Virginia,** sells appliances, bedding, cabinets, and grills. Owner PJ Orsini says, "If you use it, and if customers eat off of it, they will buy it." The Orsini's store features a purpose-built indoor-to-open-air patio for grilling demonstrations and customer interaction (*eating*). There are cameras mounted around the grilling area for livestreaming and posting content online.

There are endless opportunities to design remarkable experiences.

Understanding that people want experiences is the first piece of the puzzle. Next it's up to you to brainstorm ideas that will work, build an experience, test it, and continue refining it to make it better.

THE EXPERIENCE SUPERSTARS

Jordan's Furniture in New England has been in business since 1918, and Eliot Tatelman, the current president and great-grandson of the founder, Samuel Tatelman, is without a doubt one of the most creative people in retail today. Jordan's has seven stores reaching from Portland, Maine, to New Haven, Connecticut. And these are not your average stores.

When you visit a Jordan's location, you see a great selection of indoor and outdoor furniture, but you also see restaurants, ice cream shops, laser light shows, dancing waterfalls, indoor ziplines, rock walls, Imax theatres, and more. Sure, they want you to buy stuff, but as their mission statement says, "It's all about the experience." If Willy Wonka were to open a furniture store, this is exactly what it would look like. (Minus the boat ride from hell, of course.)

Eliot and his team have created a culture at Jordan's that starts with a profound appreciation of their own people. According to Peter Bolton, Chief Operating Officer, "If we take great care of our team, they will take great care of our customers." That's the kind of thing companies like to say, but their team lives it every day. Jordan's wanted to do something nice for the staff working in the 850,000-square-foot distribution center, so they hired an ice cream truck to drive through the facility, blaring that classic ice-cream-truck music and handing out treats to everyone in the building. At the annual meeting the leadership team made themselves targets in a dunk tank. Another year they put on harnesses, hung themselves from a lift, and turned themselves into human piñatas.

While other companies are figuring out ways to cut costs and take advantage of their employees, Jordan's is looking for opportunities to rig things in their favor. How about a bingo game where everyone has a similar card and gets bingo and the prize all at the same time? Or when they dropped over sixty thousand Ping-Pong balls from the ceiling to announce their annual five-figure bonus for all employees? When Jordan's says, "It's all about the experience," they apply that thinking to their own people as well. Bolton says, "We try to create a culture of happiness. A high morale leads to a much better customer experience, and we're all about that."

Jordan's is known for their innovative approach to business, and this is easy to see when you are shopping for a bed. If you need a new mattress, you can find a sleep shop or mattress store in New England, no problem. Or you can go to Jordan's and get fitted for your new mattress by one of their Sleep Lab experts. They are easy to find; just look for the people in white lab coats. During a typical mattress shopping experience, you walk into the department, lie down on a few beds, find one in your price range that feels good, and set up delivery. Not at Jordan's. Your Sleep Lab expert will measure you, using their exclusive system called BridgeIT, which uses lasers to profile your body form and weight displacement so that it can recommend a mattress that matches your exact sleep profile and price range. Does it make a difference? Sure it does. The competitors sell mattresses; Jordan's fits you to a bed best suited for your body so you can improve your sleep and live a better life. They are playing a different game from everyone else, and because of it, they are getting different results. Much better results.

According to Peter Bolton with Jordan's, if you want your employees to serve your customers well, then serve your employees well. Make sure your leaders push a broom and load a customer's truck alongside warehouse employees. Don't be afraid to hire people who are smarter than you (or smarta than you if you live in Boston). Send handwritten notes to people to celebrate long-term employment or to console a team member over a family sickness or death. Value emotional intelligence over IQ. Believe that a big title enables you to do more for other people. Give big bonuses at Christmas, and no matter what, have fun along the way.

Eliot leads a culture that inspires creativity, which helps build incredible experiences customers will talk about and come back to. This connects Jordan's to the community. So what do they have to show for it? Mattress retailers are fighting every day to fill their stores with people. They look to their advertising and promotional offers when things slow down and wonder where all the people are. Meanwhile, Jordan's Sleep Lab experts are so busy that they have to give out pagers to their customers because they can't get to them all when they enter the department.

Chapter Five
Defining Your Brand

George and Doris Samaras own the only mattress factory in the state of Maine. In the back of the building on Marginal Way, the good people at Portland Mattress Makers hand-layer and stitch each product and sell them out front or through one of their other two stores. It's a factory-direct model: George's team makes and sells each mattress.

I met George back in 2014 because he was interested in tapping into the brain trust available through Leggett & Platt's marketing and creative department. George was a Leggett customer, which gave him access to all the assets Leggett created to support manufacturers and retailers.

During some long conversations, George told me the story of buying Portland Mattress Makers and how the company had been in business since 1938. The people of Maine are hyper-focused on buying local, he told me. For hours and hours we talked. I asked questions and took notes.

George felt his company lacked a specific identity. The Portland Mattress Makers brand wasn't defined and he didn't have a clear vision for how to define it. He was constantly asking, who are we?

For many years George had appeared on television with a giant pair of scissors and had promised to cut out the middleman and save customers money. It was a strong message. Only a factory-direct business could eliminate markups from manufacturers.

The advertising worked for many years. But the market had shifted and George noticed larger retailers that could beat him on price moving into the neighborhood. The competition drove George to start evaluating his business's competitive strengths and figuring out how to use them to his advantage.

George needed a well-defined brand people understood and trusted. He needed to carve out a unique position in his marketplace, and he needed vivid messaging and visuals to communicate that position.

When we distilled down the market conditions and the competitive advantages, Portland Mattress Makers had two key elements working in its favor. Customers wanted to buy local, and George had the only mattress factory in Maine.

I hopped on a plane and flew to Portland to visit George and see the operation firsthand.

George's factory and showroom had a hometown boutique feel. The factory was intimate and packed with mattress materials. The showroom had high ceilings and was easy to navigate. Tracey, who worked in sales, was friendly and knowledgeable and told me about her love for horses.

After chatting for a while, I sat back and watched. George had told me his typical customer was an educated female in her early fifties with a higher income, who preferred buying locally made products. Sure enough, a woman matching this description walked in and started talking to Tracey. "Where do you make your mattresses?" she asked. "Right behind this wall," Tracey said, pointing toward the cinder blocks separating the factory from the retail space.

Later that day, I urged George to knock down the wall and install glass garage doors that allowed people to see into the factory. I didn't want another customer walking into the store wondering where the mattresses were made.

At that moment I became convinced of the brand and the position and how to communicate the message vividly. The *factory* must be the focus.

When developing a brand, people often start with mission, vision, and values. They'll use a lot of flowery language that sounds good at first but when applied to the specifics of the brand comes off as lukewarm.

I call that hollow language.

Words like "quality," "value," and "service" don't inherently mean anything. You must prove what those words mean to your company. When you use vivid examples, you paint a crisp picture in people's minds. You don't want to require your audience to fire up the full power of their imaginations to figure out what you mean by *quality*.

For Portland Mattress Makers, we had to focus on being local and prove the business was local with a vivid image: the factory.

We decided to weave together a brand vision using the factory as the backbone. The main messaging and visuals would feature the factory, and we created a tagline to drive home the angle.

Provided by Portland Mattress Makers

When you visit PortlandMattressMakers.com, the main image features the Sleep Local tagline with text that reads, "In our tiny Portland factory, we have been building mattresses by hand since 1938."

Below that message is a button linked to the factory page—the vivid, living example that proves Portland Mattress Makers is truly local.

Here's a snippet of copy from the website that captures the approach of highlighting the company's local focus and the factory:

> In a world where many people don't know where their products are made or how their food was grown, we are proud to continue a tradition of mattress making that started in 1938, right here in Portland, Maine.
>
> Our factory is more than machines, springs, foams, and fabrics. It's a maker's studio where local men and women craft the comfort that helps you live a better life. It's a humming hive of activity where we pour our passion for better sleep into each and every mattress.

No matter where you buy a bed, start your journey by touring our factory on Marginal Way in Portland. We will answer all your questions so you can make an informed decision and get a fair deal.

Once we'd created the brand and developed a vehicle for telling the story, Portland Mattress Makers was off and running. They had an identity. They had a unique position that would be difficult for competitors to knock off. They had a position that built value in their products and kept them from having to play pricing games.

The new brand—including a logo, tagline, color palette, and website—rolled out in early spring. We shot new TV commercials and created a video entirely dedicated to the factory.

The timing of the launch gave George and his team enough runway to begin telling their story to customers while giving the new message time to pick up traction.

After the Memorial Day selling season passed, I called George for a status update. He said business for May was up 25 percent over the previous year's record month. In the past, they'd always advertised a mismatch sale in May. This year, they didn't run a single promotion. They had built their unique brand and were telling their story.

Under the banner of the new brand, George decided they weren't going to have a sale. Customers still came into the store. They were enamored with the locally made products that fit with their personal identity as people who support local businesses and want to buy high-quality home goods.

It worked. And since then, George has expanded his operation to support a growing business.

It wasn't easy. The brand development process took at least a full year. George did the difficult work of taking a deep dive into his business and emerged with a clear and manageable vision to execute.

This process can be scary and frustrating. But it's worth it because you'll uncover who you are and how to fearlessly communicate your identity.

(That's enough from Kinsley for now. From here on in this chapter, we're back to the collective wisdom of Dos Marcos!)

Developing Your Identity

Each day across America, garbage trucks barrel and bounce down city streets. Metal claws emerge from these steaming trucks and turn blue plastic cans upside down like bullies shaking coins from kids' pockets. Trash collection is common. It's a necessary function of society. So what would encourage a company to try and make it fun?

Smart marketers may look at this commodity transaction and imagine how easy it would be to disrupt the garbage business by adding personality and fun. That's exactly what happened in Western Oregon.

Western Oregon Waste, or WOW, was born when a disjointed family franchise decided to do it differently. All the franchisees operated under different names. There was no efficiency in ordering graphics for trucks, and there was no central identity.

In Jon Spoelstra's book *Marketing Outrageously*, the author writes about WOW. In an effort to align the franchisees, the company rebranded as Western Oregon Waste. A big comic-book-looking WOW! was painted on the sides of trucks. The team created an actual comic book featuring a superhero who told customers about hazardous-waste handling, extra garbage pickup, and how to get their garages cleaned without lifting a finger.

The WOW brand was built around fun. It stood out from the bland trash services in most cities. And the changes made an impact. Extra services generate approximately 10 percent of revenue for most waste management companies. After the rebranding, WOW brought in double that amount. Their garbage collectors didn't have to race from house to house to increase efficiency. Their staff didn't have to work longer hours.

WOW's brand guided their positioning and messaging. From the get-go, by defining their brand in a way that stood out, marketing assets were infused with an element of fun that attracted attention and led customers to use more of WOW's services.

Since rebranding, WOW has been sold to Recology. Why did we use an example of a brand that doesn't exist anymore? Because without having a unified brand and a clear identity, many businesses aren't sellable. WOW made itself scalable and sellable, both signs of a healthy business.

It all maps back to creating a brand.

Haunting Questions

Nationwide Marketing Group's Mike Whitaker works on behalf of thousands of independent retailers across the United States. He notices themes. Common problems. As we noted earlier, most of these map back to three key questions retailers need to ask and answer.

Who are we?

What do we do?

What do we believe?

These questions provide clarity and give business owners like James Perez something meaningful to talk about.

James Perez owns fourteen Mattress Firm franchise locations in South Texas. As a boy, he rode around on a flatbed pickup truck, selling mattresses door-to-door with his dad.

One summer, James decided to start a lawn-mowing business to earn extra cash for school. As in those days on the flatbed with Dad, James went door-to-door asking if people needed their lawns mowed. And people kept saying, "No, we already have someone."

James went back to his dad and said he needed to find a new neighborhood. People weren't buying.

"What are you saying to people?" his dad asked.

"I'm asking if they need their lawn cut," James said.

His dad suggested a different route. "Are you going to college?"

James shrugged, "I hadn't thought about it. I guess so."

"Well, if you're going to college, I'm not able to pay for it, so you better save up some money. Where would you go to college?"

"Texas A&M, I guess."

"Those are Aggies. That's landscaping. That's what you're doing right here. So what are you going to name your company?"

"I guess Aggie Landscape," James said.

"Next time you knock on a door, tell them what you're working for. That you're working to get into Texas A&M. Show them you named your business Aggie Landscape, and let's see if you find any yards that need to be mowed in the area."

James followed his father's advice. The next thing he knew, he was mowing every single yard in the neighborhood. Texas pride swelled as people saw a young man working hard toward something great. These new customers told their neighbors the story of the kid mowing lawns with plans to go to Texas A&M. Job after job flowed James's way.

James's father taught him the importance of telling his story and communicating his purpose. Who are we? What do we do? What do we believe? James checked the boxes beside each of the three key questions, and people connected with his story.

Have you asked questions such as Who are we? Do we have an identity? Does this all feel disconnected to anybody else, or is it just me? What should we be known for?

These questions swirl and sway and often remain ignored.

Amazon CEO Jeff Bezos said your brand is what people say about your business when you're not in the room. Gary Friedman, CEO of Restoration Hardware, puts it this way:

> "People camping out for days in a line to be the first to buy a new phone, when they could have easily ordered one online is not rational, but they do it. It's a customer saying: 'I believe what you believe.'"

When a feeling of disconnection bubbles up in business owners, it's often a sign of maturity and a pending breakthrough. You're beginning to realize the value of a cohesive brand and how alignment of certain elements can impact your business.

Many companies flail and flop like a carp on a dock. Put me back in the water, they say. Have I ever been in the water? I'm still flopping around with a hook in my mouth. This is awful!

To develop your brand, we are going to take you through a process that includes positioning, message, and identity.

Personify Your Company

Start the brand development process with a fun exercise designed to assess your starting point. If you don't have a sense of the current state, you'll have a difficult time getting on the right path and finding the finish line.

Ask yourself, if our company were a person, who would it be? We'll give you two paths to personifying a business.

Pick a Celebrity

This is the shortcut route. If your company were a famous person, who would it be? Are you hip and current, connected to the youth, and operating in urban environments? Maybe your brand is Bruno Mars. What if you're structured and suave, running a tight ship that looks like a disciplined football team? Your brand might be Tom Brady. Or, if you're in a rural part of the country surrounded by storytellers and farmers, maybe your brand is Miranda Lambert.

Personification Exercise

A deeper-dive method involves asking questions to describe your personified business. Here's a list to get you started.

Your business is a person:

1. Are you a male or female?

2. What's your age?

3. What's your annual income?

4. What do you drive?

5. What genre of music do you listen to?

6. Describe your house.

7. Describe the clothing you wear.

8. What do you eat for breakfast, lunch, and dinner?

9. How many kids do you have, if any?

10. What's your favorite hobby?

11. Where do you vacation?

12. Talk about your religion or spiritual practice.

These questions will reveal a person. Now, write a thick description of this person. Or write out their typical day, starting with breakfast and ending with bedtime.

In doing so, you'll create a person who represents your current brand.

Do you like who you are? Do others like you? Do others know you who you are, or have you kept your true nature hidden?

Like any personal transformation, the personification of your brand helps you get to know yourself so you can create a plan for growth and change. Now, with this clear image in mind, we'll begin the process of developing your brand.

It starts with writing your mission, vision, and values. Your mission is your purpose. Vision is where you want to go. Values are your nonnegotiables.

Mission, Vision, Values

If you have mission, vision, and values, jot them down. Never been through this process? Staring at a blank piece of paper? Below are examples to get you started.

Mission: _____.

Our mission is to provide comfort to all through the products we sell and by serving people in our community.

Vision: _____.
In five years, we will be the number one seller of mattresses in our market.

Values: _____.
Integrity. Honesty. Creativity. Service.

Don't skip this process. Do the work. Dog-ear these pages and make sure you complete the steps. If you fail to define the purpose of your business, the direction you want to go, and what you stand for, your company will flounder.

Once you've identified your mission, vision, and values, you're going to wade into territory that most people miss—culture.

Culture

Evaluating your culture is critical to defining your brand. During this step, you will talk to management, employees, and customers to understand how they view the business and the current state of your culture.

Another option is to conduct surveys among your employees and customers. Gathering anonymous feedback online can make respondents feel safer, making it more likely they'll be candid. There are many tools available, including Google Surveys, Betterworks Engage, and Nationwide Retail Insights.

Ask employees questions such as:

1. What words would you use to describe the culture around here?

2. What are our team's biggest strengths and weaknesses?

3. What do people in the community say about us?

4. What's the strangest thing about working here?

5. What's missing from our business that would take us to the next level?

6. What else?

7. What else?

8. And what else?

When you're gathering feedback in person, don't forget to ask *what else* and be quiet. You'll get some gold after those periods of awkward silence.

Once you've talked to employees, management, and the delivery staff, find customers to interview. Not your friends. Real customers.

Ask customers questions such as:

1. What would you tell somebody if they asked what our business does?

2. What are we the best at, or known for, in the community?

3. What words would you use to describe our employees?

4. What do people around town say about us?

5. What are some stories you've heard about our business?

6. Are there needs we're not fulfilling? If so, what are they?

7. Describe your ideal shopping experience.

8. What's missing that would make our business better?

9. Would you recommend us to your friends? If so, why? If not, why not?

10. What else?

11. What else?

12. And what else?

Gather this feedback and take a hard look in the mirror. Do the responses match with who you want to be?

Be brutally honest in asking, who are we? Your culture *is* your brand. At every touchpoint, your people are branding the company.

Let's say your vision is to become a tech-centric mattress seller that looks like the Apple of the bedding business. Sounds like a cool vision, but first you need to look at your employees, your current culture, and the state of your business. Can your people work with a brand built around tech? Or do they schedule appointments on a PalmPilot and barely get out of bed in time for work?

Failing to define and design your culture will torpedo your brand before it's ever brought to life.

When you evaluate your culture, you might find it's not how you want it to be. At this point, you might decide to begin changing culture or instilling values in your people that deepen the definition of what your business stands for.

During the culture piece of this branding process, you may find there's work to do before you begin building the brand of your dreams. Now is the time to do that work, not later. Your people must be aligned with the brand, or customers will smell inauthenticity and trust will evaporate.

Brand

Whether it's retail or product, brands are important because consumers are navigating a complicated world where they encounter up to ten thousand ads every day.

Brands become filters for decision-making. If you're looking for a piece of furniture and you know Pottery Barn's style fits your vibe and their quality is good, you'll shop there first.

That brand clearly stands for something in your mind, and you'll filter out all the other options and place Pottery Barn at the top of your where-to-shop list.

If your brand stands for nothing, you won't be used as a filter.

The focus of this final section will be your brand position and pillars. These will become filters you can use to make business and marketing decisions.

Positioning: There Was No Third

Charles Lindbergh was the first person to fly solo across the Atlantic Ocean. Do you know who was second? The second pilot to solo the Atlantic flew faster than Lindbergh and used less fuel. He was faster and better. What's his name? Almost nobody knows.

If you aren't able to guess the second person to fly solo over the Atlantic, you're probably thinking there's no way to guess number three.

That's because there wasn't a third person—there was only the *first woman*, Amelia Earhart.

In the book *The 22 Immutable Laws of Marketing*, Al Ries and Jack Trout argue, "The basic issue in marketing is creating a category you can be first in. It's the law of leadership: It's better to be first than it is to be better."

Amelia Earhart wasn't third. She created a new category and is known as the first woman to fly solo over the Atlantic.

Many companies try to be better and faster, like that second guy to solo the Atlantic, whose name was Bert Hinkler. Instead of attacking a market and being first, like Amelia Earhart, these follower companies often let the leader emerge, then hop into the fray with a better product or one with their big corporate name attached.

A stronger position is doing what Anheuser-Busch did in response to Heineken. They decided if there was a market for premium imported beer, there was likely a market for premium domestic beer. The Anheuser-Busch team created a new category in which they could be number one. Michelob beer was born and became the number one premium domestic beer.

In what category can you be first, or number one? How can you *Amelia Earhart* your own category? To develop this position, you'll need to evaluate the competitive landscape.

If you run a mattress store, you'll need to gather a list of competitors and determine how they're positioned in the market. Many of these competitors will lack definition. Some will be "family-owned," which means nothing if the public never sees the family. Others will advertise themselves as mattress stores with brand names. Again, a big, fat nothingburger with a side of empty sauce. Don't let their lack of creativity define what you do.

What can your business be the first to do?

The first mattress store in the tri-state area? Maybe. If that's the truth.

The first store to guarantee same-day delivery? You'll need to narrow inventory, stack it deep, and find staff willing to work late. But you can do it.

The first Tempur-Pedic elite retailer. The first luxury mattress store in town. The first jungle-themed furniture shop on the planet. The first furniture store with a concert venue. Think firsts. Brainstorm a big list, step away for a day, then narrow your selection and choose a winner.

DOS MARCOS TIP

> Brainstorming should be dedicated to generating as many ideas as possible. Go for volume. Brainstorming is not a place for criticizing or selecting ideas. Gather a team and HATCH ideas (see page 99). Tell your group their job is to generate ideas, not criticize. Build on each other's thoughts. Set a clock and try to get as many crazy ideas on a whiteboard as possible. Once you've exhausted your creative juices, step away and get at least one night of sleep before you come back to evaluate your list and select a winner. During sleep, your brain connects current experiences to past knowledge. It unleashes creativity that isn't available on demand.

George from Portland Mattress Makers chose a position his business could own: the first and only mattress factory in Maine. If he'd followed the leader, George would have tried to sell lower-priced products.

George did the deep work to understand his culture and the attitudes of his target audience. All those inputs informed the positioning, messaging, branding, and creative execution. It all worked together. That's branding. When your promotions magnify your brand instead of interrupt it, you're doing it right.

Marketing expert Seth Godin said that specificity is a form of bravery. Keep in mind, your position might be specific, but that doesn't mean it's the only thing you do. It's the main message. All things are *no* things. Say too much and people hear nothing. Say one thing and people hear much more.

Pillars

In early 2019, I signed on as President and CEO of the Englander mattress company. For 125 years, Englander had been producing quality mattresses in a range of price points.

As a licensing organization, Englander operated eleven factories across the United States and produced different products in each territory. There was no consistency. If Susan living in California loved her Englander mattress and wanted to recommend the same bed to her mom in New York, there was nowhere for Mom to find that product in the Big Apple.

The Englander board recognized this issue and knew it was hurting business. Our retailers wanted a more robust digital presence for the mattresses they sold in their stores. By building a consistent national line, we would be able to feature products on our website and establish trust with consumers who were doing product research. It's basic business these days, but, saddled with legacy issues and having experienced consistent business success, Englander hadn't pulled the trigger on moving into the modern era.

As I evaluated the opportunities and challenges, it became clear the Englander brand needed to be refined and defined.

I spent a couple of months traveling and talking on the phone. I visited our retail customers and spent time with our sales reps. A theme emerged. Our customers said Englander was known for making comfortable mattresses that are built to last. That's good, I thought. We have a reputation for high quality.

Others told me Englander was known for latex mattresses. Digging deeper, I discovered old advertisements co-branded with Goodyear. In the 1950s, Englander was owned by the Goodyear Tire & Rubber Company, and that relationship provided access to rubber foam formulations. Back then, Englander called latex "airfoam." Englander was the first brand of any significance to place latex in a mattress.

Englander was known for quality, had a solid heritage story, and was recognized for using latex, a unique and proven component. But I found out something else—over and over again, retailers and reps pleaded for us to keep it simple. Products should be easy to understand. Marketing should not confuse consumers. Keep it simple.

With all these inputs planted in my brain, I gathered a team and began the process of refreshing the Englander brand. It started with our mission, vision, and values. Luckily, the board had done a great deal of this work prior to hiring me.

Next I focused on culture. My travels gave me a clear view of our people and retailers on the front lines selling Englander mattresses. The process of listening and learning was about defining reality and understanding the cultures connected to the company—our culture and our customers' cultures.

From there, we benchmarked our brand in relation to the rest of the mattress industry. Instead of simply looking at our usual competitors, the agency we hired did their own research and came back with a report that entirely focused on direct-to-consumer online brands like Casper, Tuft & Needle, Purple, and DreamCloud. The agency argued that, to consumers, the trade brands didn't matter. The trade brands didn't show up in online search and were therefore invisible to mattress shoppers. That was true. We decided to benchmark our brand off those with online visibility because most consumers researched or shopped online.

With competitive landscape in mind and notebooks full of rich feedback from our audiences, we began outlining who Englander was going to be. We wanted to create brand pillars that guided our decision-making. Understanding retailers' desire for us to keep it simple, the mattress industry's reputation for being confusing, and our own desire to make quality products, we discovered our brand pillars—*simple, transparent, best inside and out.*

Those pillars informed the product line we launched and the aesthetic of our Las Vegas Market showroom, and of course they mapped to all the identity elements of our brand, such as font styles, color palette, and the logo refresh.

Each decision we make now gets filtered through a single question: is this simple, transparent, and best inside and out? If not, we rethink it. Those guideposts keep the brand from making low-priced commodity products. That's not us. The brand pillars tell us where to go. If a marketing piece is complicated, we rework it. We know simple isn't always easy, but we keep after it until simplicity emerges.

Defining your pillars allows you to align your team around ideals that tell you where to go and sometimes what to do. You won't have to fight to figure out if a merchandising decision or advertising piece fits. Filter those ideas through your brand pillars and you'll often get easy answers to questions causing you to stall out.

(That's enough from Kinsley for now. Next, we're back to the collective wisdom of Dos Marcos!)

Bringing the Brand Forward

All this deep work is designed to bring your brand to life in its messaging and visuals. Your store and your website will hold hands. Your marketing materials will look like they belong with your website, and your social channels will have a voice that fits your culture. Done properly, these things all work together to form an identity that deepens your connection to consumers.

At this point, if you don't have a business name, logo, and tagline, that's okay. The process we've taken you through will give a design team the information it needs to create a compelling name and logo. And with all those creative juices flowing, you can brainstorm a big list of taglines, go to sleep, come back to that bank of ideas, and select the winner.

Building a brand takes intention. Competitors can easily rip off products, but it's nearly impossible to steal a brand that's built around pillars, principles, and people. Your brand can create a wide moat around your business that's filled with alligators and serpents. The dirty-window-store guy won't even try to swim across that gurgling swamp.

When your brand is ready, it's time to develop creative assets, such as videos or digital ads, and distribute those ideas to your audience. This is when your hard work comes to life in the form of ads, images, point-of-purchase materials, social posts, and videos.

Unlike zany promotions that often uncouple your audience from your brand, the new ads, ideas, and initiatives you create will complement the brand you've developed. Promotions will magnify your brand rather than interrupt it. The in-store experiences will look and feel connected to the digital ads your audience sees on Facebook. We want to create a swirling ecosystem that feeds itself and expands your planet.

All this brand work builds a strong foundation for the house that sits on top. If you don't plant those pillars deep into the earth, your house could shift and sway. It might collapse in a stiff breeze. We want your brand to be strong enough to weather a hurricane because the strength of that house will be known to all.

Let's recap. To build your brand, you're first going to personify your business. From there, you will determine if this caricature matches who you want to be. Next, you'll talk to employees and customers to figure out what people think about your company and gain a clear sense of culture. Then you'll use this perspective to develop mission, vision, and values; define culture; and create a position you can own in your market with an effort toward being *first* in a category.

Congratulations on deciding to do it differently!

Now it's time to build a business around your brand and start making money. In this next section, we'll show you how to develop clear goals, strategies, and tactics—they're all different, and each serves a distinct and important purpose.

Then we'll introduce a surefire method for brainstorming and developing creative ideas that match your brand, plus explain how to produce messaging around those ideas.

But we won't stop there. We'll give you a roadmap to help you guide the creation and deployment of your marketing. Let's do this!

Chapter Six

Goals and Creative Process

C had Crenshaw and Davis DeRock are a Kansas City–based comedy duo whose on-camera antics first found their way into the mattress industry in 2010. Chad, a jovial guy with expressive eyes and a shock of curly hair, played the role of Gary in *The Virgin Mattress* web series. That means Chad got two paychecks—one for the original version that was canned and another for the reshoot.

These two writer-actors popped into my head shortly after I became responsible for the Leggett & Platt Bedding Group's marketing. The company was facing a significant opportunity with an innovative innerspring product that wasn't gaining traction. We needed to rethink our approach and cut through the clutter. Mattress manufacturers weren't biting. The product was called Quantum Edge. It delivered multiple benefits to consumers, retailers, and Leggett's customers, mattress manufacturers.

After evaluating the product and conducting market research, I decided it was time to rethink our approach. There was no documented strategy. Interviews and inputs from our target audience were nonexistent. A creative hook and a simple marketing funnel were nowhere to be found. I believed the product represented an entirely new category of bedding components and that a positioning strategy would be key to market penetration.

Once we'd finished planning, we needed to grab our audience's attention with something fun and unique, take the side door into people's minds when nobody was looking, and get people to laugh and listen. Once we'd done that, we could use humor to talk about the benefits of the bedding component and drive people to a site where they could learn more and get connected with a sales rep.

Before diving into the fun side of marketing, we had to ask some tough questions and truly understand the lay of the land. Why were mattress makers not rushing to adopt a component that offered multiple benefits and could save them money? We had to go to work on better understanding the problem.

Quantum's Edge

Up until that point in the bedding industry, many mattresses were made with foam encasement. Imagine a thick picture frame made of foam and with an innerspring unit inside. That's foam encasement.

Leggett's bedding component product, Quantum Edge, was a replacement for foam encasement. Quantum Edge brought narrow coils all the way to the edge and kept mattress manufacturers from having to make a foam picture frame that bordered the spring unit. It created a consistent sleep surface and kept people from feeling like they would roll off the mattress. It solved real problems.

A survey of retail sales associates (RSAs) showed the edge of the mattress comes up during 93 percent of sales interactions. A lot of RSAs said if a consumer sits on the edge and doesn't like the feel, they won't even lie down and try the mattress. The big issues shoppers brought up were roll-off and consistent sleep surface. They'd say, "I don't want to feel like I'm going to roll off" and "I want the mattress to feel the same from side to side."

The benefits kept stacking up.

We talked to factories and found that, by using Quantum Edge, mattress manufacturers could improve their factory flow. Inside a mattress manufacturing plant, glue stations are a big bottleneck for production. To make foam-encased mattresses, assemblers glue foam rails to a piece of base foam. This assembly and gluing process tends to take a significant amount of time compared to the rest of the mattress-making process. With an edge-to-edge innerspring, there's no need to build foam tubs. The Quantum Edge unit was all one piece.

If the Quantum Edge component solved problems for consumers and manufacturers, why was it not picking up traction? The answer revolved around the fact that change often meets resistance.

To adopt Quantum Edge, manufacturers would have to change the way they were building beds. Those foam edges were built to hide the coil heads and make the sides of a mattress look smooth and tailored. With a coil stretching to the edge, the mattress would need a thicker border panel or a vertical quilt line to keep a coil from scalloping out the side.

More resistance would come from the front lines. Retailers would have to change the way they sold higher-end mattresses. For years, salespeople had told consumers foam encasement was great. They'd have to change that message. Plus, if they continued carrying mattresses with foam encasement, they'd need to figure out how to explain the benefits of Quantum Edge without trashing their foam encasement products.

Beyond the hesitancy among our customer base to adopt something new and different, some of Quantum Edge's lack of traction was our fault. There was no clear goal and there were no strategies in place. We didn't understand enough about the mind frame of our customers (and their customers, the retailers). We needed to crystallize the goal, develop a plan, and create attention-grabbing marketing that built value in the product. To do this, we educated ourselves about the market, developed the plan, and called the kings of mattress comedy, C2D2—Chad Crenshaw and Davis DeRock.

The Method

The process we used was simple and repeatable. Keep in mind, just because something is simple doesn't mean it's easy. This approach can produce results, and it takes a lot of hard work.

We'll take a deeper dive into the process later in the chapter, but let's start with how we applied it to Quantum Edge. It begins with five steps:

1. Identify the opportunities and challenges.
2. Learn from your audience.
3. Set goals and develop strategies.
4. Develop creative and marketing.
5. Launch in all channels.

To tackle the Leggett challenge, we first asked, "In a retail setting, is there any conversation about the edge of a mattress?

If so, what's being said?" Our research showed the edge came up during nearly every sales interaction. Customers hated a weak edge. Retailers told us many shoppers wouldn't try a bed if the edge felt flimsy. Foam encasement sometimes didn't have the same firmness as the innerspring unit inside. Customers didn't like that inconsistency because it felt like they weren't able to sleep on the whole mattress. Boom. We had valuable intelligence to feed our goals and strategies.

Next we documented our goals and developed strategies. For the Quantum Edge campaign, we set a goal to increase the number of customers buying this product in the next twelve months by a specific percentage. For customers already using Quantum Edge, we set goals for increased volume.

Our strategies revolved around explaining the cost savings to manufacturers and getting retailers to ask suppliers for products featuring Quantum Edge.

Next, creative and marketing. This is where it gets fun. There are an infinite number of ways to add sparkle to an explanation. With a clear plan in place, you can unleash the creative beast and brainstorm a campaign that supports each strategy and accomplishes the goals.

When thinking about the differences between Quantum Edge and foam encasement, the old Mac versus PC commercials came to mind. Those ads featured a hip young guy wearing a hoodie and jeans standing next to a stodgy middle-aged guy in a tweed blazer and slacks.

One of the spots begins with PC sneezing. "Gesundheit," Mac says, handing PC a tissue. PC says he has a virus that's going around. "You better stay back, this one's a doozy," PC says. "Last year, there were 114,000 known viruses for PCs." But Mac isn't worried because those viruses only affect PCs.

The Mac versus PC campaign forced the audience to see the

world as if only two choices existed. This or that. Us or them. The ads masterfully highlighted distinctions between the two products. This method, we thought, would work for us. Flimsy foam encasement versus strong Quantum Edge.

After a big hairy brainstorm, the Edge Heads was born. Chad and Davis took the lead on writing scripts, and we decided to produce a series of snackable, fun videos that adopted the spirit of Mac versus PC.

The Leggett Labs team constructed a hollow mattress with two face holes located at opposite edges and slots for each actor to stick an arm out. The two edges would occupy the same mattress, but in their adventures, they would experience different outcomes.

Provided by Leggett & Platt

In the six-video series, which you can see at MattressEdge.com, Quantum Edge sails through life as a strong and confident component, while Foam Encasement struggles to stand up to the demands of life on the edge.

The Results

We pushed the videos and the website into the industry and supported the campaign with detailed marketing material that highlighted our edge-focused retail research, the benefits of manufacturing with Quantum Edge, and our scientific tests showing our product was 26 percent more durable than foam encasement.

As we blasted the message into the industry and promoted the videos on every available channel, we mobilized our sales team to push the message with a strong ground game. They visited factories, had fun showing the videos to customers, and reignited the discussion about the benefits of Quantum Edge.

Placements picked up. Customers started using the product. As we gained momentum, we realized Quantum Edge represented a bigger category of products.

The human brain processes things categorically. When you think, "Who flew across the Atlantic?" it doesn't go through a roster of names. There's no "Who did it best?" It only thinks who did it first. This is why we tend to substitute brand names for product categories. Kleenex is a brand of facial tissue. Band-Aid is a brand of adhesive bandages. In Houston, you ask for a Coke and the waitress will ask, "What kind?" In parts of the South, Coke has become a term for a whole category of soft drinks.

In the mattress industry, Tempur-Pedic owns the category of memory foam mattresses. For many years, Craftmatic meant adjustable base.

Knowing how the mind works, we wanted to turn Quantum Edge into a category. Since our edge product was active and responsive, we named it ActivEdge and launched a variety of products under this umbrella. We created a new category. When you create a new category, you become first in people's minds. And when you're first, it doesn't matter who comes along and tries to do it better—they'll always be second in the audience's mind.

In a typical mattress, those foam encasements we were trying to replace take up 18 percent of the bed. For a large company like Leggett & Platt, that meant 18 percent more wire and springs inside each mattress. The results: tens of millions of dollars in new business that didn't cannibalize any existing sales.

The process of creating goals and strategies that lead to creative outputs and deliver results—it works. Follow these next steps and get ready to start pumping in the profits.

(That's enough from Kinsley for now. Next, we're back to the collective wisdom of Dos Marcos!)

Goals, Strategies, and Tactics

Imagine standing at the base of a fourteen-thousand-foot mountain and saying, "Hey, I think I'd like to reach the top." You scan the towering mound and see a switchback path. It looks like the path runs into a sheer cliff face. Beyond the cliff there's a scree field that bleeds into a large ring of snow surrounding the summit.

As you evaluate the situation, a donkey saunters down the ramp of the helicopter you chartered up to the base of the mountain. You're carrying a pickax, climbing equipment, and a backpack with gear, clothing, food, and water.

Your goal is to get to the top of the mountain. How you get there—your strategy—is up to your imagination and the resources available.

You could take the helicopter. That's the easiest approach. Load up, fly to the top, and climb down the dangling ladder. But that doesn't sound fun. That's not who you are. You want to experience the adventure and the satisfaction of trekking up the side of the great mountain. Your decision to go by foot reveals something about your values; your brand is showing its face.

If there were a winding path, you could ride the donkey to the top. But your assessment of the mountain tells you that's not possible. That strategy alone won't work, so you decide to combine several approaches. The terrain is varied. You decide the donkey will accompany you partway up the path. Then you'll load up climbing gear to ascend the sheer face and pack a jacket to stay warm near the summit.

You're combining strategies to accomplish the goal. Each strategy will come with tactics. Think of tactics as the tools you need for each phase of the journey. The donkey, climbing gear, warm clothes, food, and water are all tactics. If you estimate the journey will take twelve hours, you'll need to pack enough food and water. If you're traveling when it's dark, you'll need to bring a headlamp. By thinking through each strategy, you can make a list of what's needed. This framework also applies in business and marketing planning.

Goals are what you're aiming to accomplish. Strategies clarify how you're going to approach the goal. And tactics are the items you need to support each strategy.

- Goals = What
- Strategies = How
- Tactics = Create

Goal Setting: Get SMART

When things go wrong, they usually go wrong at the beginning. If you don't know what you're working toward, it's difficult to stay focused and impossible to measure your progress.

Goals are critical to your success. Even if you fail to reach your goal, you'll gather intelligence. You can use that intelligence to debrief, learn, grow, and adjust future efforts.

When putting together goals, use the SMART framework:

- Specific
- Measurable
- Achievable
- Realistic
- Time-based

Groups tend to flounder and fall apart when pursuing goals that are pie-in-the-sky. "Change the world" is an admirable aspiration but a terrible goal. It's too vague. A better goal is "Decrease homelessness in downtown Austin by 10 percent within the next eighteen months."

That's a vivid goal. It's specific and measurable. It appears achievable, and it's relevant to your mission to change the world. There's a timeline in place. This goal fits the SMART framework.

As with climbing that mountain, when your goal is set, there are many ways to achieve it.

Strategies

Let's hit the pause button. Remember all the work we did around identifying and developing your brand? Don't forget who you are and what you stand for. Your brand shapes your strategies. Goals are concrete and cold—increase top-line sales 30 percent in Q2. Meanwhile, strategies feel a bit warmer and add some definition to your plan.

A good strategy meets three criteria:

- It's relevant to the goal.
- It's connected to your brand.
- It contributes to achieving the objective.

Let's break it down so you understand how to generate strategies without getting tactical—"Design a print ad" is a tactic, not a strategy. It's not time for tactics yet.

Imagine you have a mattress store and decide you want to increase sales 15 percent over the previous year. You write down your goal: "During the next twelve months, increase sales 15 percent year over year." What are the best ways to achieve that objective and magnify your brand? The list is endless. Let's say you conduct a brainstorm session—we'll lay out a framework for that too, later in the chapter—and decide that the best ways to increase sales are:

1. Surprise and delight our customers to increase word-of-mouth referrals and improve online reviews.
2. Introduce sleep accessories into every selling opportunity.
3. Demonstrate adjustable bases to every customer who enters the store.

Those are strategies for how to get 15 percent more in sales. Once you've captured those strategies, it's time to develop the creative approach and come up with tactics you can deploy to support and amplify each strategy.

Tactics

Now let's break down tactics attached to one of our strategies.

- Strategy:
  - > Surprise and delight our customers to increase word-of-mouth referrals and improve online reviews.
- Tactics:
  - > Each RSA will learn a magic trick and perform it at the close of each sale.
    - · Buy a magic trick.
    - · Set aside time for each person to practice.
    - · Have each RSA perform the trick in front of team before showing customers.
  - > Send customers a rubber chicken with a funny note that requests a review.
    - · Buy rubber chickens.
    - · Develop mailers for customers.
  - > Ask customers for reviews and let them know you're donating ten dollars to Boys and Girls Club for every review, good or bad, during the month of October.
    - · Contact Boys and Girls Club for donation approval.
    - · Create a handout to give store guests.
    - · Train sales team on properly communicating this request.

Each tactic maps to the strategy. Sending customers a rubber chicken with a note has a high chance of surprising and delighting them. A decent percentage of people will probably talk about it and follow instructions to leave a review. A magic trick can have the same effect.

When you observe the connections and differences between goals, strategies, and tactics, you see how the three build a solid structure for attacking opportunities. That's the high level. Now it's time to get granular.

How do you cook up those creative ideas?

And how do you get the most out of each of them?

Read on!

Chapter Seven

Getting It Done

Creativity doesn't happen on its own. And once it does happen, you need to channel it to get the most out of your ideas. That's where we're headed now, starting with the creative process.

Dos Marcos HATCH Creative Method

Creative thinking is critical when it comes to setting yourself apart from the competition. For some, thinking outside the box comes naturally, and for others, it's tough.

Look around your town. How different is one oil-change business from the other? Do florists in your community have unique personalities? How about your HVAC folks; do any of them stand out?

If you're a creative thinker, keep up the good work. If you lack creative juices, we have a process that will HATCH big ideas. Bring together a good group, use the process, and watch the ideas flow. This is the path to making your business stand out so that you get paid.

What you need for this exercise:

- A quiet room away from any distractions. Consider going off-site.
- Giant paper, like a Post-it Super Sticky Easel Pad with some wall space to hang.
- Colored markers.
- Nickel-sized round dot stickers in different colors. You can get these from an office supply store. Purchase twenty stickers in each color, and have enough colors so every member of your team has their own color.

Before you start, do something fun to get people in a positive state of mind. Play a game, have a Nerf-gun war, or watch a few funny videos. According to research by Leigh Thompson at Northwestern's Kellogg School of Management, telling an embarrassing story at the beginning of a brainstorming session caused groups to generate a greater volume and variety of ideas. Talk about that time a plate of spaghetti fell on your head. Vulnerability often increases likability and makes people more likely to build on your ideas.

Now it's time to apply the HATCH method:

- Hold a brainstorm
- Act crazy
- Take a nap
- Choose ideas
- Hand off to creative team

Hold a Brainstorm

Clearly define the objective. Decide what you are trying to accomplish, and be specific! Increasing sales isn't a goal. Increasing sales over the Labor Day holiday by 10 percent over last year is more like it. After you figure out your goal, write it at the top of the Post-it pad to keep things in focus.

Act Crazy

Select a group of no more than five to seven people. They need to have a positive outlook on life, work well with others, and have some unique perspective on how your business runs. No people with lame negative personalities—not even if they are the boss; they will ruin it for everyone! Set the expectation right from the start so everybody knows the game they are about to play. No idea is a bad idea. No criticism after an idea is floated. The goal of a brainstorm is not to select ideas, it's to generate a large volume of them. We recommend adopting what improv comedians call the "Yes, and" method. When one actor introduces an idea to the audience, the partner actor always builds on that topic. The second actor never shuts down the first actor's idea. If one actor is pretending to be a sweet old grandmother who breathes fire like a dragon, the second actor would never say, "No, be a grandmother who breathes ice." That approach kills the momentum. Using the "Yes, and" method, the second actor would think, "Yes, and the fire-breathing grandma has to sing in the church choir this Sunday!" Tell your team of brainstormers about the "Yes, and" approach and keep each other committed to the process.

Another framework we like to use is the twenty-idea method. Start spitballing ideas, and don't stop until you get to number twenty. After about ten ideas it gets tougher to conjure new thoughts, but that's also when things start getting good. When you push past the obvious, you get to the surprising ideas. And after all, "Surprise is the foundation of delight," as Roy H. Williams said. Stupid stuff gets said, laughter ensues, and creative juices start bubbling.

Take a Nap

Step away. Close out the meeting, go home, get a great night's sleep, and come back to your brainstorm list the next day. It's remarkable what happens when you allow your brain to process new material overnight. When your unconscious mind marinates on ideas and new inputs, your brain creates connections in your subconscious.

English actor and comedian John Cleese, who co-founded Monty Python, attributes a great deal of his creativity to working on a problem, sleeping, and returning to the material.

Regroup and hand out colored stickers so each person has their own color. Then have each team member go up to the Post-it pad and place a dot on their top-five favorite ideas. You can expand it to more than five if you want, but the goal is to force the best ideas to the top of the list.

Choose Ideas

Bring back your team and focus on your top two ideas. Make sure you all agree that these are the best of the twenty; check to make sure they have the most potential.

It's time to start putting together your strategy and thinking about the best way to execute it. How will you measure success?

What will the budget be? What are the deadlines to meet the objective? What should the return on investment be? How can you fail? How can you mitigate that failure? What are the tactics you will have to employ to get the desired outcome, and who are the best people to assign those tasks to?

Hand Off to Creative Team

Hand off your newly HATCHed ideas to the creative team and let them begin bringing it all to life. That's where we're headed next.

Before we go there, do a post-game analysis on each brainstorming event. Is this something you will do again? If so, how can you make it even better? Discuss what the group did right and what you need to do differently next time.

The Dos Marcos Galaxy Graph

Ever had something like this happen? A team member says, "Let's create a print ad!" A week after the ad hits publications, somebody says, "Let's produce a video to match that print ad. And we should do some digital ads." On and on it goes. Sure, you're pulling levers. But your tactics keep trickling and dripping. Don't do that anymore. It's costing you time and money.

That same scenario, the gentle oozing of tactics, used to happen to us all the time. Highly inefficient. You could have done all that creative work at once. Plus, by virtue of the video and digital ads being afterthoughts, you should be asking, what else should we have created to match the print ad? Are there other channels where we can push the idea and increase exposure? Is there an opportunity to create an in-store experience around that idea or develop an engaging social media promotion?

The trap of underdeveloped ideas snares lots of business owners. An idea inspires your imagination. You want to launch it into the marketplace. Your brain chooses a channel that feels familiar, like newspaper or television. It's easy to imagine what the idea will look like in that medium, and you round up the team to start creating content.

What you should be doing is atomizing that one idea and pushing it into every channel. We call this the Galaxy Graph. It's an easy way to force yourself to create assets for every channel you own, bring in the right people to support the execution, and make sure you don't end up looking back on a promotion, wishing you had done more to make the strategy work. Remember that when things go wrong, they tend to go wrong at the beginning, so look comprehensively at each strategy to avoid missing opportunities.

Once you begin developing tactics to support your strategies, you should be pulling out your Galaxy Graph worksheet and determining every single asset you need to create.

Each time you're ready to create a campaign or an idea bubbles up to the surface, go through your Galaxy Graph line by line. Circle each item you need to create. Like a pilot's pre-flight checklist, the Galaxy Graph keeps you from having to remember everything. It's easy and effective. It forces you to fully develop your ideas and use all your channels to maximize exposure.

Take a look at this typical Galaxy Graph and think about how many channels you would have left off!

PUBLICATIONS

Print ads

Digital ads

Partner for a promotion

Email blasts

Press releases and
media coverage

SOCIAL CHANNELS

Content to post

Survey / poll

Contest for fans

Digital ads

Personal outreach to fans

Post to other groups

PUBLIC RELATIONS

How can this idea
become news?

Create in-store event

Article for publication

Partnerships with other
businesses

INFLUENCERS

Promotions

Giveaways

Blog posts

Social media posts

Digital ads

Partner with other businesses

TELEVISION AND RADIO

Spots

Digital ads

Partner for a promotion

Email blasts

Press releases and
media coverage

WEBSITE

Home page update

Landing page

Blog posts
or articles

INTERNAL

Communication to employees

Sales-team training and creation
of selling materials

Email signatures adjusted
to campaign

Legal considerations

Communication needed throughout
the campaign

Notify other divisions and partners

Update all website properties you own

GENERAL CONTENT

Digital ads

Print ads

Email marketing

Blog posts or articles

Videos

Press releases

Use this worksheet before you start creating marketing assets to ensure you don't leave out anything you need. Every time you have a big idea for which you develop goals and strategies, pull out a fresh Galaxy Graph and circle all the assets you can create for all channels of distribution. Remember that you won't circle everything on your Galaxy Graph every single time. Pick and choose the best tactics for each individual promotion.

This process forces you to maximize each idea and create all the assets at once so they work in tandem.

Well Done!

Now it's time to sit back and pour a tequila shot, the official beverage of the *Dos Marcos* podcast. Toast your team and start counting the profits from your new initiatives. It's important to find a way to celebrate each win because these moments of reflection and smiles will inspire what's really important for your business—people working in a culture that celebrates creative thinking!

You now have the framework for developing goals, strategies, and tactics. You have a surefire process for surfacing wild ideas and making them match your business objectives and your brand. And you even have a simple worksheet to help you firehose those unique ideas onto all the places where they can make an impact and help you connect with consumers.

Next, it's time to start pulling levers. Sounds fun, right? We're talking about word-of-mouth marketing, reviews, social media, digital, selling process, and public relations. When you build a brand and roll out a rock-solid plan, pulling these levers is like hitting triple sevens at the casino. It's jackpot time.

Chapter Eight
Making It Rain

Knowledge is only potential power. It becomes power only when, and if, it is organized into definite plans of action, and directed to a definite end.

—Napoleon Hill

By now you should understand the importance of:

- Deciding to do it differently!
- Connecting to people in a way that makes you the preferred place to shop.
- Building a compelling brand and using the CAGE method to identify opportunities to serve and delight your customers.
- How to HATCH creative ideas that connect to business goals.

We've talked a lot so far about the "what" and the "why" of driving traffic and business to your store. Now let's talk about the "how."

Large e-tailers and big-box retailers have giant budgets. It would seem they have the advantage over you. But maybe not. The size of your spend is only part of a sound traffic-driving strategy. The other part is what you say, how you say it, and where you say it.

Most retailers get into an advertising groove. They run the same promotions year after year with the same media outlets. When foot traffic doesn't boom and sales numbers stagnate, they wonder why the business isn't growing.

When pushing a promotion into your market, you should take a more holistic approach, using all your channels of influence.

We will focus on seven key levers you can pull to create interest and excitement around your store and products. When you sit down to plan your next event, take out your Galaxy Graph and think about how to pull *every* lever:

1. Traditional advertising
2. Word-of-mouth marketing
3. Consumer reviews
4. Social media
5. Selling process
6. Public relations
7. Your website and digital presence

Pull one lever and you can sell some products. Pull them all and WATCH IT RAIN!

Advertising: Sales or Substance

How warm and fuzzy do you feel watching an ad promoting a two-for-one deal on a chicken sandwich? It might signal a better deal on chicken, but it's not going to connect you to the people in your community.

In 2008, Chick-fil-A was facing tough competition from other fast-food restaurants that were giving away items for free to create spikes in business. Giveaways may generate some traffic, but it's short-term thinking and brutal on the bottom line.

Chick-fil-A decided not to participate in a price war. Instead, they created Daddy-Daughter Date Night. Jeff Rouse, owner of a Chick-fil-A in Olathe, Kansas, wanted to host an event that would drive people into his store and give dads and daughters a memory that would last a lifetime.

Little girls put on their best dresses, dads wore suits, and they stepped into a fast food restaurant that had been transformed with soft music, white tablecloths, and fresh flowers on every table. The event was such a smashing success, Chick-fil-A stores all over the country adopted Daddy-Daughter Date Night and added red carpets, carriage rides, and strolling violinists. It has since grown so big that community members now volunteer to help make it a special night for everyone involved.

Competitors were advertising discounted chicken. Chick-fil-A was advertising the opportunity to deepen the connection between fathers and daughters.

The biggest mistake retailers make when it comes to their advertising is getting stuck on product-price-and-promotion messages. If that's where you focus, where do customers place their attention? Is a transaction the only outcome you are after?

There is no reason you can't use advertising to hook your audience while also *building value* in your products, process, and people. If all you do is scream "SALE" during every major event, you blend in with every other business. You become noise that's easy to tune out.

Carve out space to talk about something cool you're doing in your community. Imagine a television ad with twenty seconds spent building value in something special or telling a story, coupled with a ten-second pitch about the offer. That format still works, and you'll accomplish way more than your bland competitors will, doing what they have always done.

You see two digital ads scrolling through your Facebook feed. One screams discount, the other tells a story and makes you feel something. Who's playing the long game?

Having trouble thinking of what to say? Dip back into the CAGE model in chapter 4 and look for those opportunities to create Community, offer Answers, Give, and design Experiences.

Chick-fil-A advertised Daddy-Daughter Date Night instead of a price-focused promotion. It's an event their restaurants can repeat several times each year, and it has become so popular, they have to take reservations for the evening. When we see that Chick-fil-A cares about our family enough to create this sort of event, it connects us to them in a special way.

Important! We're not saying that you shouldn't run promotions, but if that's all you're doing, then you're missing the real opportunity. We think it's pretty incredible that people running a fast-food place started a tradition for families in their community. You can do it too; just put some creative muscle into it and see what happens.

Word-of-Mouth Marketing

According to invespcro.com, word-of-mouth marketing, or WOMM, drives $6 trillion of annual consumer spending and results in five times more sales than a paid media impression. Their research has shown that 88 percent of consumers place the highest level of trust in recommendations from the people they know. WOMM is even better than customer reviews because it happens organically.

In chapter 4, we discussed Jordan's Furniture, one of the

most impressive retailers on the planet. Warren Buffett knew what he was doing when he bought this company, because there aren't many like them. Check that. There aren't *any* like them.

Eliot and Barry Tatelman wanted to build a business that not only sold stuff, but also delivered an experience so good you couldn't help but talk about it when you left. Jordan's visitors post pictures of their kids flying through the air on their zipline and upload selfies with giant animatronics in the background. Take a look at the following conversations between two friends texting each other about what they did that day. Which conversation excites you more?

Bridget: So what did you do today?

Tara: Not much. Finished up some work then I had to go shopping for some new bedroom furniture because ours is so old and ugly! Not a great way to spend my day, but we found something we really like.

Or...

Bridget: So what did you do today?

Tara: Well, I finished up some work and then went to this place called Jordan's Furniture to buy a new bedroom set. Have you been there? This place is insane! I took my nieces and nephew, and they LOVED IT. We watched a laser light show, had homemade ice cream in their little shop, and the kids never complained once. Oh, and we found a new headboard and mattress, which we love. You have to take Gabby and Nick there; you guys will have a blast!

We know not everybody can duplicate this sort of experience! But you can give your customers something to talk about if you make the effort.

Whenever we launch Spink and Co. beds with a new retailer, I tell the RSAs the same thing: it's not likely that your customer will go to a cocktail party later that night and tell their friends they bought a new mattress from you. But if you sell them a Spink and Co. bed that is incredibly comfortable; is made with wool, hemp, and linen grown on a three-hundred-acre farm in the countryside of Yorkshire, England; and has been celebrated by the Queen, then you have a legitimate chance of someone telling that story. With select retailers, after the customer has purchased their bed and a few weeks have gone by, I send them a box of Thumbs gourmet cookies from Minneapolis and a thank-you card for choosing our bed. How often do you get a nice gift in the mail to thank you for buying something? Would you be more likely to tell your friends about the Spink and Co. beds after enjoying some rosemary pecan cookies with a cup of afternoon tea?

What are you doing for your customers that is so good they'll want to tell their friends? Go back to the CAGE section and see if there is something you could implement to make yourself unforgettable.

Your people, products, store experience, and what you do in your communities are all things people could talk about. To get people to share your stories, you have to excite them, and to do that, you have to think outside the mattress box. Word-of-mouth marketing is earned, not given. Use the HATCH method, get creative, and look for a chance to wow people.

(That's enough from Quinn for now. Next, we're back to Kinsley!)

Consumer Reviews

On a Saturday afternoon, I was browsing at a store for trail-running shoes. I found a pair that looked nice. Rugged outsole. The liner and tongue looked comfortable. And the brand was familiar. And yet, as I stood there holding the shoe, I found myself wondering if I even wanted to try it on. Sure, it looked nice and checked all my initial boxes. But I thought, "Even if it's comfortable, how do I know it's going to last?" There were no reviews on the shelf. And after doing a quick search, I couldn't find any online reviews.

How could I be sure the shoe was a good purchase if I didn't know what others thought? I was hungry for some objective opinions. Human beings have always been interested in others' thoughts and experiences. Those can be highly persuasive.

In Robert Cialdini's classic book, *Influence*, he writes extensively about the six principles of persuasion, including the ever-powerful social proof: "We determine what is correct by finding out what other people think is correct." The principle of social proof is the reason internet reviews are one of the most powerful forces shaping consumer behavior.

(That's enough from Kinsley for now. Next, we're back to the collective wisdom of Dos Marcos!)

The Power of Reviews

In 2008, Michael Magnuson went shopping for a mattress and got frustrated when he couldn't find any credible reviews. Most of the products in stores weren't listed online, and the ones that were had virtually no reviews. He later discovered manufacturers gave the exact same mattresses different names so their retail customers couldn't be cross-shopped.

Magnuson wanted reviews. He was craving third-party perspective from actual customers to help him make a purchase decision. Sensing a shared frustration from other mattress shoppers, Magnuson decided to solve the problem by creating GoodBed.com, now the largest consumer mattress review site on the internet.

The GoodBed team reviews mattresses and collects reviews from verified owners. Their videos and written reviews offer extensive analysis of a variety of aspects relevant to mattress shoppers.

Magnuson gave us a series of tips on how retailers can harness the power of reviews to build trust with shoppers.

Tie Reviews into the Bigger Brand Picture

Customer reviews should reinforce your brand position. Your store reviews had better substantiate the claims you've made. If you position your business around convenience, a significant number of customer reviews should back up this claim.

If you're struggling to find a place to plant your stake in the ground, look at your existing reviews and find out what people are raving about. Those positive reviews can guide you to what you're already good at so you can add fuel to the fire.

How to Get Reviews

The two best ways to get reviews are:

- Ask
- Make it easy

If you're a successful local business, chances are high that your average customer is a happy customer. Unfortunately, though, the average customer won't bother to leave a review if anything gets in the way of them doing so. On the flip side, an unhappy customer will go out of their way to submit a review because they're angry and want to vent. This is why you need to invest in a process that generates reviews from *all* customers. If you leave reviews to chance, you'll end up getting a sample skewed toward negative feedback.

You can overcome this skewing by getting more people to write reviews. Don't just try to get happy customers; encourage everyone to leave a review. Many retailers are afraid to ask everyone for reviews because they want to avoid negative feedback. They are often scared of reviews because of the high proportion of negative reviews they've gotten to date. What they don't realize is that their choice *not* to ask all customers to review has given their few unhappy customers an outsized voice in their online reputation. The reality is that unless there's a fundamental issue with your product or business, you'll be fine. You will attract positive reviews that would have never surfaced otherwise. Ask everyone and make it easy.

How do you make it easy for customers to leave a review? Find a channel that can't be ignored. Text messages, for example, or providing customers the ability to submit reviews from within emails through a service like Podium. The reviewer never leaves their email dashboard. Eliminate log-ins. Those are a barrier. Digital requests work better than analog ones, since they can link to where the customer can post their review. Making a customer type in a URL to leave you a review is another barrier. Conduct user testing. Map the review journey. Reduce friction. Test and see what produces the highest yield.

STORE REVIEWS

Don't ask for people to leave a review while they're in your store. That feels wrong. But do contact the customer immediately after they leave your store.

By contacting a customer while the experience is fresh in their mind, you're more likely to generate a response and get rich and colorful information about that person's experience.

PRODUCT REVIEWS

Gathering product reviews immediately after the purchase is virtually worthless because the customer hasn't experienced the product. Target thirty to ninety days, which gives people time to try the product. Timing your review request to arrive shortly after the trial period ends (based on your return policy) may help you get feedback mostly from customers happy with their purchases.

Also, your customer service team can follow up with a call. That sends a message that you stand behind your products. Your service person can tell the customer, "We care about our customers' long-term satisfaction with the products we sell, so we've partnered with the leading independent mattress review platform, GoodBed.com, to collect feedback that will really help other consumers looking for a good mattress."

Prepare your customer service team because:

- You'll get a lot of positive feedback you never would have seen.

- You'll get some negative feedback you never would have seen.

When you do get negative feedback, it's an opportunity to *wow* that customer with amazing service and turn a hiccup into word-of-mouth marketing. Invest in preparing your customer service people with empathetic responses and plans for making things right.

How to Use Reviews: Don't Take Our Word for It

Reviews are assets. You can deploy them in your marketing. They can be used to encourage your team. They should be used to make your business more credible and trustworthy.

Reviews are also third-party validation for any claim you make. Anytime you make a claim, follow it up with, "Don't take our word for it…" and then fill in the blank with a review that substantiates the claim.

If you say, "Our mattress store is the most convenient place to shop," then you'd better have customer reviews that say things like "I picked up the phone at 11 a.m. and by 3 p.m. I was lying down in my bedroom on my new mattress. I can't believe how easy it was."

Consumers are fairly cynical and guarded. They don't believe what companies say and often doubt claims as soon as they hear them. Reviews give them a reason to believe.

Where Should You Collect Reviews

Even retailers who have done some of these things often make this common mistake: they focus their reviews on only one or two websites. This would be fine if every single one of your prospective customers only went to those sites when deciding where to shop—but this is not how consumers shop. You need to have a positive online reputation *everywhere* your prospective customers are looking.

It's not enough to only have reviews on your website or Google. Spread them around. Once you've earned a sizable number of reviews on one platform, the next review on that platform is less valuable to you than the first review on another platform. For example, once you have one hundred reviews on Google, ask customers to post reviews on Yelp, Facebook, and GoodBed.com. Reviews on GoodBed can also be syndicated back to your website, providing a double benefit for every review and giving more credibility to the reviews your website displays. Consumers become aware of your business through a variety of channels. That's why it's important to pepper each path with plenty of reviews to prevent any one channel from looking like a ghost town.

Read, Read, Read Product Reviews

Product reviews are a huge part of the customer journey. Salespeople need to read product reviews, or they'll never earn the trust of today's customers. By the time shoppers come into the store, most have done research. If your team doesn't know *at least* what your customer knows, how can they credibly position themselves as experts?

Well-schooled salespeople can also proactively recommend helpful online resources to their customers. For example, GoodBed provides objective video overviews of many product lines to offer a third-party perspective. Many stores have found this content helpful as a sales tool and a training tool.

Before you can guide the customer to new information, you need to start by meeting them where they are. This includes making sure your team is familiar with complaints posted online about the products you carry.

Evil Review Sites

Reviews pack so much power that scammers have flooded the space. In the mattress industry, these sketchy bloggers figured out how to game search engines and get in front of unwitting shoppers.

As you work to generate reviews for your business and the brands you carry, it's helpful to understand the review-related content consumers are coming into contact with while searching online. Unfortunately, untrustworthy mattress review sites are rampant, and shoppers in your store will likely come into contact with these sketchy blogs. Use this information to educate your team and your customers.

If you search Google for "mattress reviews" or "best mattress," a variety of spammy websites appear. The people who run these sites understand how to rank high in search results for keywords related to mattress buying. Many sites are actually owned by mattress companies. These affiliate sites post biased reviews that endorse products for which they collect a commission.

This is big business. Millions of dollars flow through these websites.

Here's an example of how the relationship between a mattress brand and a spammy review site is structured. A consumer searches Google for "best mattress 2020." In the search results, they find what appears to be a credible website, visit it, watch video reviews, and click a coupon link under one of the mattresses. Once the shopper clicks that affiliate link, they're redirected to the mattress brand's website. When the shopper completes the purchase using that trackable affiliate link, the mattress company sends a commission check for $150 to the owner of the review website.

In many cases, there's no incentive for these review sites to post unbiased information. Their goal is to drive web traffic to mattress brands offering the biggest commission and get unsuspecting consumers to purchase. Because they only make money when a consumer clicks their links and buys online, the one thing all these websites agree on is that their readers should never buy a mattress in a brick-and-mortar store. They perpetuate negative stereotypes about mattress shopping to convince customers they would be foolish not to buy their mattress online. Your salespeople need to be prepared for many (if not most) of your customers to have been subjected to some of this messaging before they come into your store.

In an effort to advocate for consumers and shine a light on the sketchy nature of these review sites, GoodBed.com maintains a list of sites with ties to mattress companies. GoodBed also publishes information on how to spot shady mattress review sites. This is important information for your salespeople to have in order to credibly explain to customers why those websites can't be trusted. According to GoodBed, there are several easy ways to spot an untrustworthy mattress review site. The clearest signal is the use of "best mattress" lists. Any real mattress expert knows that choosing the right mattress means finding one that meets your unique needs, preferences, and priorities across a variety of criteria. Even narrowing by sleep position or mattress type is not enough. As a result, any list of so-called best mattresses is misleading, and any website that publishes such a list has revealed itself to be untrustworthy.

For these websites, these best mattress lists are their most lucrative pages, allowing them to put the brands that pay them the most money in the top-rated positions. A customer may think they've done their homework by identifying a brand that consistently appears in best mattress lists, but all they've actually done is identify a brand that consistently pays spammy websites the most money.

Social Media

When companies first started investing in social media, there was a big debate about whether or not it could deliver any results. How can a Facebook post with kittens curled up around a bottle of Tide sell laundry detergent? There was some legitimate pushback over this, mostly because social media was a new medium for advertisers and the traditional channels didn't want it taking any ad dollars away from them.

While naysayers were pooh-poohing social media, a wild man from New Jersey named Gary Vaynerchuk started posting videos on social media in which he tasted and talked about wine.

His profile grew and he became known as a social media guru. He would speak at corporate events and drop f-bombs. He was all over the internet, ranting about the importance of social media.

Many self-styled gurus come across as marketing hacks trying to drum up business, but Vaynerchuk was genuine and persuasive as he sat on stage and told this story: he was in a deep discussion with the CEO of a large company, and she was pressing him to tell her the real ROI of a social media investment. After trying to explain it a few times, he finally turned it back on her and said, "Tell me, what is the ROI of your mother?" She said, "Excuse me!" and Gary said, "Uh-oh."

Vaynerchuk explained that he wasn't trying to be disrespectful. He was asking a legitimate question. "I can't sit up here with slides and say to you that when I was in the sixth grade and came home with a mullet and my mom said that I was gorgeous and could do anything I wanted to do in life, that was building self-esteem and because of that I sold a few more cases of wine at Dad's liquor store, which allowed me to expand the business. I can't show you that map of her influence, but I can tell you that I'm going to buy a multibillion-dollar sports franchise someday, and it's totally because of the impact my mom had on my life."

Social media is a storytelling platform. The cost is low, but the investment of time is not. Social channels are probably set up in your business. These channels support images and video content, and you can use them to interact with everyone in your universe. If you tell a story that makes people feel something, you build a connection with your audience that will drive their decision-making.

Would you have ever thought a company could get you excited about a cooler? Consider the example of Yeti. Yeti manufactures coolers. They are really awesome coolers. Like all coolers, they keep things cold. If you go to their Facebook page, don't expect to see pictures of Yeti coolers with copy talking about how much colder things are in a Yeti than in a competing cooler. There are no sales or promotions pushing you to retailers that carry their products.

Instead, there are stories like that of Raph Bruhwiler, Canada's first pro surfer, who was raised in the deep woods of Vancouver Island. There's even a video of Raph on a journey to a remote location chasing that perfect wave—with his Yeti, of course. It's not about their product. It's about getting people excited about using the product on a dream trip.

Social media is an incredible way for you to talk about how your grandfather started your business. It creates the perfect opportunity to do profiles on your own people and talk about how your business would not be what it is today if not for the crazy efforts of your team.

You can produce video reviews of the latest and greatest products so your audience understands how special your products are compared to the junk your competitors carry. It's a way for people to interact with you and see if yours is the kind of company they want to trade with. But best of all, it's a way for you to show your customers the true heart and soul of your business. If you dip back into what we covered in the section about CAGE in chapter 4, you can begin to see how you can bring some of that to life using your social media accounts.

Feature a story about a charity you support. Remember our advice from earlier: it won't feel like bragging if you make it about them, but be sure to include yourself in the story. When consumers know that you are focused on more than the bottom line, you will become their preferred place to shop.

Selling Process

Now that you have done all of the work to get people into your store, what are you going to do with them? If you asked one hundred customers what separates your business from the competition, what would you hear? Whenever working with retailers, we ask what makes them different from the competition, and the most popular response is "Our people set us apart." This may be true, but it's not always enough.

Think about it. You haven't purchased a bed in years, but now you're in pain because your mattress sucks. You start doing research online to educate yourself on what bed is going to be best for your body and your budget.

Big problem, though: this is way more confusing than you thought. After you battle through all the sales, promotional messaging, fake online reviews, and pushy salespeople who are only after your money, you realize that this process is much harder than you imagined.

Our friends at Mattress Warehouse understand the in-store experience they deliver has to be unique in order for them to be the go-to for great sleep, so they follow the bedMATCH process. The bedMATCH diagnostic system uses eighteen statistical measurements and thousands of scientific calculations to identify the mattresses that provide the best postural support for individual body types. You lie on the bed, they hit the magic button to measure your body, and out comes a mattress recommendation based on your height, gender, distribution of weight, lumbar curve, neck pain, back pain, and so on.

At this point, you realize that this retailer is actually trying to uncover your needs and fit you for your perfect bed; they want to *help* you, not just *sell* you. This gives Mattress Warehouse something to build value in through their advertising, cool stuff to talk about on their social media, and an experience worth sharing in a review or with a friend. But the real reason it works is because the process requires the RSA to asks the consumer questions about their sleep, which ultimately builds trust—and trust is the key to the sales process.

By this point in the shopping cycle, hopefully your customers have read great reviews about you, heard from their friends about your awesome customer service, discovered through social media that you share the same passion for fighting child hunger, and watched you promote it all with radio and television advertising. The consumer is primed and ready for the "moment of truth" when they actually come face-to-face with your business and experience your culture and your salespeople. Will this moment mirror what they've already learned? Some salespeople ask customers what they are looking for and immediately start showing their best products. The Mattress Warehouse sales reps ask lots of questions and have great listening skills. When the consumer feels you really care about them and their needs, you build trust and have a better chance at winning a new customer.

Think about ways to customize your selling process with a unique promotion. If a certain percentage of your proceeds goes to one of your favorite charities, have a nice picture board in the front of your store that highlights all the good things that group is doing in your community. If a consumer does an official test of your featured item, maybe they get a special discount offer or, better yet, one of Grandma's homemade cookies. Tell me and I'll listen. Show me and I'll watch. Involve me and I will buy. Don't just sell your customers; have fun with them. If your current shopping experience and process are just like those of your competitors, then there is huge potential for you to connect with your customers in a more compelling way.

A typical selling process involves some form of the following steps. Your job is to make sure your brand and your creative ideas come through in the process.

1. Establish trust and connection.
2. Discover needs and wants and map to solutions.
3. Create a memorable win-win outcome customers want to tell their friends about.

Final thought—it's pretty obvious when you're shopping for a product and the person helping you is in it for the commission. The next time you have a sales meeting, ask your team members what they do for a living. If they tell you they sell mattresses and furniture, tell them they are in the wrong place. Help them uncover the real purpose behind what they do. Most consumers don't really understand the importance of sleep, nor do they understand that buying a new mattress could change their quality of life. When your salespeople realize they are in the life-improvement business and every "up" they get on the selling floor is a chance to help someone sleep better and live better, their motivation will change and your sales will increase. We all know what it feels like to be on a car lot or in a retail store and be *sold* by someone working toward a big commission. We also know what it feels like to work with a sales consultant who is focused on helping solve a problem. Those are two very different experiences that will get you two wildly different results.

Public Relations

Public relations can bring a lot of people to your front door. It's probably one of the most underutilized traffic drivers. It's also called "earned media" because you don't pay for it, so it's important to offer something newsworthy when you reach out to the media for coverage. Strong relationships with your local media will make all of the difference, so when you're reading your newspaper, watching television, or listening to the radio, make some notes on who does a good job covering local events. You can also connect to local influencers who may blog about your community or do some cool stuff on Instagram or YouTube.

Jim "Mattress Mack" McIngvale from Gallery Furniture in Houston, Texas, is one of the best at generating free press. And as we told you earlier, after Hurricane Harvey destroyed people's homes and many had nowhere else to go, Mack opened his doors, providing refuge for hundreds who were displaced.

MASTER CLASS FROM MATTRESS MACK

As "Mattress Mack," Jim McIngvale of Gallery Furniture has become famous for his big bets. Beyond the millions of dollars in press coverage, there's a deeper layer of genius at work. In 2019, Jim promised customers who spent $3,000 or more a refund if the Astros won the World Series. The event generated foot traffic and press, both in good measure.

As the Astros headed to the World Series, Jim knew how much money he needed to offset customer refunds. He bet about $13 million the Houston Astros would win the World Series against the Washington Nationals. If the Astros won, Jim would win his big bets and cover customer refunds. It was an insurance policy that created more exposure. By jetting around the country placing giant wagers, Jim amplified buzz, creating more press for himself and the Gallery Furniture promotion. But it wasn't just the press that made this promotional event such a master stroke. It was also the increase in the number of times Mack's audience heard his message and the conversations each Houston Astros game generated.

Advertisers are often focused on the number of people hearing their message and how many times each person hears it—reach and frequency. Mattress Mack's bet created a built-in machine that worked in the background to generate reach and frequency; to achieve these results through traditional channels likely would have cost millions of dollars.

For customers who took the bet and spent $3,000 or more, their interest in Houston Astros baseball went through the roof.

Once a purchase is made and the novelty wears off, most people don't talk about their furniture or mattress—unless they made a bet against Mattress Mack. If you bought a couch at Gallery Furniture, every time someone sits down to watch a game, you're telling your friend that sofa might be free if the Astros win the World Series. Throughout the season, you're watching baseball and holding out hope you'll get your goods for free. This means you're thinking about Gallery Furniture every time you watch your home team. For Gallery Furniture, these are free positive impressions.

The Gallery Brand comes back to a customer's mind during every baseball game. And there are 162 games in a season!

Making Your Event Pressworthy

If you want to get some attention for your business:

1. When you plan an event, find a way to make it newsworthy. The event has to be special or unique in some way that is relevant to your audience. Having a sale with the proceeds going to a charity is a great thing to do. But if you want it to be covered by the press, make the event itself fun and interesting. Bring in local celebrities or do something wacky, like playing basketball while riding donkeys, for an unusual twist that will get the attention of reporters.

2. Get someone inside your company or hire a marketing agency to write up a great press release. Make sure you have an attention-grabbing headline, maybe something like, "Donkeys raise money for local charity." Also,

capture the meat of what you want to say early in the write-up so you keep the reader interested.

3. If you are buying advertising from a local media source, start with your contacts there. Remember that just because you're spending money with them does not mean they are obligated to cover your story. Will your budget influence their decision to "give you ink"? Hell yes it will, even if they tell you it won't! You can even bring them in on the event as a media partner, which is a great way to ensure their participation.

4. You have to know your audience. Who are you trying to reach, and what's on their mind? Remember that what's important to you may not be important to everyone. Be sure to look at your message through that lens. Consider the tone and climate of the current news cycle, and craft a news story that's relevant to your audience.

Good public relations outreach can be huge for your business. Just like word-of-mouth marketing, it involves third-party endorsements from groups telling your customers how great you are, which is *gold* to any business. But with PR, it's not just one person telling another; instead, the message goes to everyone in your city!

Website, Digital, and SEO

During the 2020 coronavirus crisis, retailers made a mad dash toward e-commerce and the internet. Retailers who'd been toe-dipping in the pool of online selling realized it was time to cannonball. Mattress stores with mediocre websites missed out. Businesses with strong websites and e-commerce capabilities witnessed the power of buying options available at a consumer's fingertips. It was a shift of historic proportions with effects that will likely change buying behavior forever.

The COVID crisis fast-tracked trends that were already gaining traction. Browsing and buying online became commonplace, even for folks who preferred shopping in stores. It's a trend that's growing and shows no signs of subsiding. That means retailers need to make long-term commitments to enhancing and evolving their websites and digital marketing.

It feels like a moving target. Changing and shifting. New tools and technology threatening to obsolete everything you've built. You need a specific mindset and skillset to excel. And that means creating a culture of creativity that attacks all things digital.

Digital marketing will change. Google will update its algorithm. Facebook will roll out new ad features. New social networks will pop up. The rapidly changing digital environment is impossible to predict, but there are principles that likely won't change. That's where we're going to focus.

Your Website Is Your Store

When it comes to the job your website is supposed to do, here's the headline: be visible to shoppers searching for solutions, and make it easy to do business with your company.

There are many ways to be visible. You can be visible and look bad. Lots of websites are atrocious.

You need to create trust. Jennifer Danko, founder of Site on Time and a division of Nationwide Marketing Group, says, "Ask yourself a simple question: based on our website, would someone shopping online have a favorable impression of our business?"

Go ask twenty strangers their impression of the business

behind your website. Tell them you're a researcher. Listen to their responses. Ask open-ended follow-up questions like, "What do you like and dislike?" Have these strangers rank the trustworthiness of your business on a scale from one to ten.

Then go to work creating a site that matches the brand you're building. This process starts with your brand work and comes to life when you develop clear goals for your website.

Know the goals behind your website. Is the site informational, transactional, or aimed at growing online sales? Many retailers want consumers to visit their store. If that's your goal, your website should create compelling reasons for the consumer to visit. If your goal is for people to buy online and pick up in a store (BOPIS), the site should be built to transact online. Give shoppers strong reasons why they should pick up items in your store (such as a free pillow during in-store pickup). Clear goals are the key to a thriving web presence.

Once your site's look and feel and your goals are firm, it's time to focus on the operational side of the website. Jennifer suggests a variety of steps outlined below to ensure your retail store is set up for success.

MATCH THE IN-STORE EXPERIENCE

Are all the options available in-store also available online? It's a simple question, but often difficult to investigate. Do the hard work. Customers expect adjustable bases, remotes, and bed frames to be available for purchase on your website. Give shoppers the ability to purchase product protection. Let them easily buy and schedule white-glove delivery—if there's an additional charge for shipping to a specific zip code, design an online experience that lets them pay that surcharge and schedule delivery. Make it easy. Every barrier to buying is a signal to consumers to bail and go somewhere that's easier to do business.

Online needs to match in-store.

SHOW INVENTORY

There are two main ways to show inventory. First, you can show *exact* inventory. This makes some retailers nervous because inventory can turn quickly. If your site shows only one or two of an item left, it creates a sense of urgency. If you don't want to show exact inventory, the second option is to categorize items as either in stock or quick ship.

When buying something they need right away, customers want to know what you have in stock. If a refrigerator breaks, the food will go bad. Someone buying a fridge needs one today and doesn't want to view items that'll take two weeks to get.

Inventory visibility increases sales and improves margins. If a consumer needs a product today, they'll prioritize availability over price.

TRANSACTIONS (BUYING THROUGH YOUR WEBSITE)

This goes back to mirroring the in-store experience. Online sales for many traditional retailers have been incremental. Years back, people never imagined buying cars online. Now it's fairly common. There are even car vending machines.

Today, people are confident making purchases online. Your job is to come up with ways to aid the customer by connecting them to the exact information they need to make the decision. For example, dimensions are a key factor for furniture and mattresses. The problem with online sales is that customers who are more apt to buy online are more likely to leave bad reviews. Call or communicate with the customer after they make larger purchases to ensure they have everything they need.

SIMPLICITY

Many retailers overthink the website design and focus on inconsequential details. Most business owners want to make their site a little different. Customers want obvious and intuitive. Product-listing pages tend to look similar across big brands because customers understand that style of navigation. Amazon is one of the least aesthetically pleasing sites, but visitors know how to navigate it.

When looking at design, make sure it represents your company and matches your branding. Then make sure it's user-friendly. Larger companies in your category have figured out designs that work. Don't think so outside the box that people don't know how to shop on your site. Don't get bogged down in small details. Look at the overall experience. Some retailers want to do "daily deals." People don't visit independent retailers' websites looking for daily deals. The customer wants to check if items are in stock; see current sales, rebates, and financing; and have a clear understanding of how delivery works.

COMPETITIVE PRICES

At the click of a few buttons, online shoppers can filter categories and find the best price. Your online store should be priced to compete. Shoppers have options. Even if you feel your exclusive product commands a higher price, put yourself in the shoes of the consumer and find out if the online shopper would pay a premium. If you're trying to sell $199 queen sets to compete against Amazon, you'll likely lose—unless you create a winning strategy to upsell accessories and increase average tickets. Prices need to be competitive. And if you're not offering the lowest price, make sure consumers understand the value added through service, delivery, financing, or other offers.

In designing your web experience, there are several other principles to embrace as you build systems. Let's look at responsive communication, preferred buying channels, targeting in-market shoppers, and channel visibility.

FIRST RESPONSE WINS

Be available in the channels where people want to communicate. Use messaging platforms like Podium to enable live chat and text capabilities. List a phone number on your website. Set up social messenger services. Give customers the ability to contact you in their preferred channels and staff those channels with people who respond immediately. When customers set out to solve a problem, like the need for a new mattress, they want to solve it in the moment. They're dedicating time now. The company that responds first wins.

E-COMMERCE, BOPIS, AND BEYOND

For retailers, selling online has long seemed counterintuitive because it's not how they built their business. Traditional retailers know that if a shopper comes into the store, the sales team can upsell and offer other items that increase average tickets. But the world has changed. Customers want to purchase in their preferred channels. They may want to visit your store, shop around, then buy from your website. Some want to buy from your website, then pick up in the store. Others choose to buy online from a trusted local retailer and have the purchase shipped to them. Your job is to make their path to purchase easy. If you don't, a competitor will.

CASE STUDY: TUCKFIT.COM

Roger Cunningham owns The Bed Store in Knoxville, Tennessee. "Our success is because of authenticity," he said. "Our slogan is, 'We'll even TUCK you in.'" TUCK is an acronym for Thoughtful, Understanding, Compassion, and Knowledge. That word and the culture it creates transcends Cunningham's mattress business. Roger and his team always want to make sure customers get the product they need, not the one with the biggest commission. He also knows customers are scared of mattress salespeople. This fear was once a barrier to purchase—and The Bed Store's website helped customers overcome it.

At TuckFit.com, a friendly cartoon character is holding a sign that reads, "Get a Free Pillow" and the copy asks, "Are you ready for the best sleep of your life?" Click the green "Get Started" button and you'll go through a series of questions related to sleep, mattress needs, budget, and preferences. The site performs "Tuckulations" to find options that fit the customer's needs.

On the final page, mattress options are presented along with a button to "Print your fit and get a free pillow!" This encourages people to come into the store. There's a video of Roger building value in TuckFit, proclaiming 97 percent of customers who use the TuckFit.com process end up keeping their mattress.

The TuckFit site also explains each mattress recommendation based on these factors: preferred comfort level, body type, sleep position, and sleep temperature. The quiz has given The Bed Store team four years' worth of data on more than seven thousand unique sleepers. This info gives insights into sleep position preferences, heat tolerance, partner disturbance levels, and much more.

At the bottom of the page, users find directions to the store, an email and phone number, and a photograph of the salesperson who works there. All this detail is there to give customers knowledge that reduces anxiety about visiting the store and opens a line of communication with the sales team. The Bed Store process also seeks to snag and serve the most important prospect: in-market shoppers. And the results are remarkable:

- Approximately 10 percent of visitors have completed the TuckFit quiz.

- Nine percent of all sales are TuckFit completions. This is based on four years' worth of data.

- Average tickets from TuckFit completions is $2,150 (that's higher than The Bed Store's average ticket).

- Of customers who have taken a TuckFit quiz and bought in-store, 97 percent have kept their original mattress and not opted for a comfort exchange.

IN-MARKET SHOPPERS

Customers have problems. They want to solve those problems and typically go online to research products that can take away their pain.

Geo-targeting allows your store to set a radius around each location and bid more money to attract shoppers within that circle who are researching products you sell. They're in the market to buy and are near your store. Set up geo-targeting and own the radius around your stores.

CHANNEL VISIBILITY

Whether it's your website, Facebook Marketplace, or Google Shopping, channel visibility ensures your products are findable along the consumer's path to purchase. Don't discount a channel because you don't understand it. Research the available selling channels, test them, and keep your foot on the gas pedal for those that work.

SURROUND SOUND

Have you ever listened to a song that starts out with a simple guitar riff, then after a while the band adds in a little keyboard, followed by a horn or two, and then some great vocals? The guitar sounded great by itself, but when you layer in the other instruments it builds into something incredible. The same goes for the levers you pull. You might be killing it with your radio spots, supported by your strong Facebook page, and making a good living in the process. But when you refine your selling process, build a better website, and sprinkle in a little public relations, you will find yourself in a full-fledged jam session, making music you didn't realize you could. Layer the instruments, get it all working together, and see what happens to your results.

Chapter Nine

The Future

"Tremendous carnage, fallout, damage done to the industry. And it will really be a resurrection—and hopefully a portal to that new digital landscape we've been talking about for 20 years."

Author and futurist Doug Stephens uttered that eerie statement on the May 18, 2020, episode of the *Dos Marcos* podcast.

Stephens is the author of *Resurrecting Retail: The Future of Business in a Post–Pandemic World.* There are many scenarios that could play out, but Doug's approach focuses on shifts in human behavior.

"I'm not focusing on waves. I'm paying attention to riptides and undercurrents that can kill you," Doug said. COVID-19 and its fallout appear to be intensifying those undertows, tugging retail down into a deep, dark ocean. The evolution, Doug says, means retail must adjust.

As e-commerce grows, physical stores must change.

Media is becoming the store. You can buy products anywhere.

Stores may end up becoming more like media outlets where brands pay for placement based on the experience a retailer can deliver to the consumer, much like how brands buy TV ads on stations that attract their target audience. Brands will want to make sure the physical outlets deliver the best in-store experiences.

In the mattress category, this approach is likely why digital-first brands like Tuft & Needle and Casper made moves toward freestanding retail. By all accounts, brick-and-mortar stores lowered local-customer acquisition costs and gave consumers a chance to experience the brand and its products.

Institutional Life

Until the mid-1800s, life as we know it today didn't exist. Most people farmed or worked in the village where they lived. Many worked for themselves or for family members. Kids didn't go off to college.

So much of life today is built around institutions. Work, education, and medicine have all become institutions and products of industrialization. Retail is a reflection of this industrialization. Stores are located along roads people drive to work. Retailers fill the street-level space below big office buildings. Stores have been placed along footpaths and roadways—anywhere people are located. But what happens when more businesses allow permanent work from home? What if 40 percent of students complete education online? It would seem those physical environments, and the retail stores surrounding them, will change or go away. Today, the store is everywhere.

The store is on your phone. The store is on the side of each website. The store is all around us. Available at any time. Even though mattresses are a more considered purchase, and something people want to touch and feel, the category still isn't safe from the broader disruption.

The mattress category experienced a layer of insulation until shippable mattresses became economically viable. That relief was short-lived, and that means retail must change. Durable goods must be marketed and sold without the customer touching and feeling them. If you can't appeal to a customer who is at home, on their device, over time your business will likely cease to exist.

What Do We Sell?

Doug says you should ask yourself a key question designed to reveal a bigger idea for your business: if we could no longer sell our products, what else of value could we potentially deliver?

In the mattress industry, the future will revolve around sleep and its benefits to all people.

Bedding retailers don't just sell mattresses. The mattress industry can sell sleep, health, and wellness, maximum human potential, and increased athletic performance. From this line of questioning and brainstorming, you should be able to find other products besides mattresses—there are services you can offer, alliances you can form, and movements around sleep you can start in your community.

Store as a Service

There are two retail paths that appear viable.

First, make it so simple to buy a product that your retail store becomes the cognitive default option. When a consumer thinks about buying your product, they don't imagine any other logos or options. Your store pops into the consumer's head because they know it's convenient and frictionless. They like you, they trust you, and they don't have to worry about overpaying.

On the other end of the spectrum is what Doug calls the high-fidelity experience. Consumers say, "I don't want a commodity product; I need a level of expertise, or I want to treat myself to an exceptional shopping experience." This could mean luxury, or a boutique retailer offering something unique. The fact that people are paying more isn't a problem. These consumers are happy to pay more, but they want something for it.

Everything in the middle is getting killed.

"It's those situations where the consumer says, you're not the most convenient, you don't have the best selection, your prices are fairly high, and you don't deliver awesome services. So why would I even bother," said Doug. "That's purgatory. That's where you literally become the place people come to search your competitor's website—in your store. That's hell on Earth in retail."

You have to prove your value. You have to choose what you're not going to do.

Store as a Starting Point

In the future, for some shoppers, the store will be the first place they experience the brand but not where they purchase. During that initial visit, they'll be exposed to the product and brought into the digital ecosystem. Later, they'll buy online through any number of channels.

There's research around the impact for online brands opening their own stores. It shows when a company that's been selling exclusively online opens a store, they experience an *online* sales increase of 27 to 35 percent.

Here's an example. The clothing company, Kippo, started out selling clothing exclusively online. When it opened its first brick-and-mortar store in Brooklyn, their website sales in the Brooklyn area increased 35 percent. While the Brooklyn store generated its own sales, Kippo experienced a boost in online orders from people with Brooklyn addresses. Customers were coming into the store, seeing Kippo clothes, then going home and buying online.

The store appears to be a starting point. Brands must ask how much they would have had to spend on digital to capture as many customers as they can with a store.

Physical stores will be a customer acquisition tool, not just a means of distribution.

Sales per square foot and comp store growth will go away. Those are products of the industrial revolution. Landlords could base rents on ratings, similar to how Nielsen shows how many people watch a TV show on a given night. If it's no longer about pushing as much product out of a store as possible, brands will want to know what the retail center is doing to bring more people into the experience. Retailers are going to look for active participation from the centers they're in.

Think about the store not as a small warehouse, but as a stage. Mattresses at a great price—not a very interesting story. Sleep and wellness impact everyone's life. Mental health. Endurance. Stress relief. More sex. These stories are meaningful and can play out on a retail stage.

The job of every independent retailer is to become *notorious*. Not just known. *Notorious*. *Notorious* for promoting health, wellness, and the life-changing benefits of sleep. To do this, you must own the category. Consumers need to think, "I can buy a mattress anywhere, but only one retailer in the market comes to mind."

There is no platform, network, or ad buy that will get you to a better place. Shifting ad dollars won't solidify you in your marketplace. You have to be remarkable.

There's too much noise. Everyone has a megaphone. The only way to break through is to get other people talking about you. Spend disproportionately on giving them not just a good experience but a mind-blowing one. Do this and you won't have to advertise.

The Gift of Reimagining

Being a little bit better than an unremarkable competitor is a road to nowhere. It's time to rethink the future and avoid the slog of sameness.

Industries make competitors more the same. We attend the same conferences, read the same publications, deal with the same vendors and suppliers, and hire the same consultants. Over time, we become more mediocre, which presents ample opportunity for disruption. Outsiders look at a lame category and can see how to gut it.

Disruption of this nature happens in industry after industry. We've experienced it in the mattress business. But today we are standing before a gift. It's an opportunity to reinvent ourselves. The post-COVID world presents a chance to completely rethink your business. Who you are, what you offer, how you offer it, and how you go to market. It's a chance to decide to be different, better, more resilient, and ultimately, more successful.

Conclusion
Our Hope for You

We hope you've been inspired by something you read in this book. By a person, a story, or a strategy that will push you down a path to do it differently. To do it better.

We hope you discover the purpose behind your business. In the mattress industry, we're in the life-improvement business. Sleep impacts every moment of every day. Our products help people sleep better and improve their health, mood, physical appearance, mental performance, and much more. We want people in the sleep space to join us in our mission to serve others and connect the mattress category to the benefits of better sleep. You may not be in the bedding business, but there's purpose behind almost every category. Uncovering and communicating why your business matters will help you connect with consumers on a deeper, more emotional level. When you create that type of connection, you'll be unbeatable.

Finally, we hope you stay connected. We love hearing from people who want to update us on their progress or have a question we can answer. Listen to our podcast at MattressPodcast. com and enjoy that cozy little campfire of ideas. Visit the site to send us an email and find our social handles. Better yet, let's meet up someday and celebrate your success with a shot of tequila and this toast: here's to great sleep and living your best life. Cheers!

Appendix One
Need a Little Help Getting Started?

When we started MattressPodcast.com, we didn't know that tiny spark would grow into a roaring campfire that people gather around to tell stories and get inspired. But that's what happened. As we've interviewed thought leaders and tackled topics affecting our businesses, we've realized the show is more than a podcast about the bedding business—it's a movement to reignite independent retail. It's a crusade to create a deeper sense of purpose and community around a category that impacts people's lives.

There's an open seat for you around the *Dos Marcos* campfire. You'll find people like you facing struggles like yours and discovering creative ways to prosper. There will be tequila shots and lots of laughing. You'll probably run into folks you want to raise a glass to. And you may even come across people you can help—people who need your ideas and support. It's a community that cares, and good people are always welcome.

The podcast is focused on telling stories and curating ideas you can implement to make your business better. Head to MattressPodcast.com and subscribe right now to hear stories from retailers and leaders who are using the ideas in this book to build their businesses and live better lives. You may be done reading the book, but your journey has just begun. Now it's up to you to change.

Change isn't easy—but we hope we've made a convincing case that it's essential for you to survive—and *thrive*—in our rapidly emerging retail world. We also hope you'll take the deep plunge into rethinking your approach as we've described along the way. But it's also important that you start *doing*, right now. Action reveals answers. Only when you take action will you see what works and what doesn't. If you sit around imagining all the possibilities, you'll waste a lot of time. Experiment with small ideas, small tests, that inform your thinking and get you moving.

Remember that crazy speech we delivered in front of four hundred mattress retailers at Nationwide Marketing Group's PrimeTime event? At the end, we asked everyone in the room to jot down a traffic-driving idea that actually worked. Some ideas are simple, while others require more polish—but all of these ideas have actually worked for retailers in the real world. And of course, we had to add some of our own ideas at the end. Stuck for something to try?

Read on!

Look at Spokane Furniture Beards on YouTube. They all have beards so they made a commercial having fun with that.

—JEREMY KLONTZ, SPOKANE FURNITURE

Created a customer appreciation day with games and food trucks.

—BEVERLY ADAMS AND FRANK MACLEAN, HOWARDS

Sidewalk sales, twelve-hour sales, and a big Christmas party.

—DAVID THORNTON, THORNTON'S HOME FURNISHINGS

Triple-play sale, choose three of the following: free box spring, free delivery, free protector, free sheets, free frame, free pillows.

—DAVE WEINBERGER

JAKE APPROVED. They use their dog Jake as a third-party endorser for products in the store.

—RON, DERANLEAU'S

We offer a 180-night trial period and created a different selling process.

—LUIS GONZALEZ, BEL FURNITURE

Created networking groups for building referrals.

—JEFF MESSLER, UNCLE DAVE'S MATTRESSES

Facebook videos using humor, history of the family.

—RON FREDMAN, UNCLE DAVE'S MATTRESSES

Girls Night OUT!!!! Put on nice event for the ladies in Ohio.

—LAURIE WARNER, RANDOLPH HOME FURNISHINGS

Reached out to local U-Hauls and apartment complexes for some cross-promotion.

—RONALD RODRIGUEZ, RODRIGUEZ HOME FURNITURE

Tailgate party with school football and drill team and chili cook-off.

—TROY SIMMONS, BEL FURNITURE

Egg Fest/grilling competition.

—BURNS MATTRESS CENTER

Wine-tasting event.

—GABRIEL ARNOLD, ARNOLD ZZZ, JOE NASHIF, US MATTRESS

Wine and recline event.

—JERRY LECOMPTE, NAPLES MATTRESS

Get involved in your community church and share the story.

—TOMMY OWENS, MATTRESS WORLD OF KERRVILLE

Donated upper-end mattresses to fire department. Got pictures and posted to social media with fire trucks in background. The fire department and all of their friends were spreading the word.

—JAMES REASONER, MATTRESS WORLD OF KERRVILLE

Bring our Amish craftsman who makes the furniture to the showroom for a "meet the builder day." Give away Amish-made cookies and homemade ice cream.

—LUCEETA ROHRER, MILLER'S FURNITURE OF LANCASTER

Team up with local gyms for an open house for gym memberships and talk about diet, exercise, and sleep as a way to live a better life.

—DAVID RIDDLE, BEDZZZ EXPRESS

Black Friday ad featuring a bed-in-a-bag giveaway for purchases of $399 or greater.

—STEVE GREENE, BEDZZZ EXPRESS

Anniversary sales, balloons for kids, serve food, free drawing, and send cookies as a thank you.

—DEBBIE, O'NEIL'S HOME FURNISHINGS AND FLOOR COVERINGS

Asking for referrals and sending email via Constant Contact asking for Google reviews.

—ASHLEY HAMILTON, DAVE'S WORLD

Put daughter in commercials since she was eight years old.

—BRIAN GARRISON

Fashion show!

—CHARLOTTE'S FURNITURE

Gave away three free beds for Christmas.

—DERREK, BEDS TO GO

Support farmers' market in our parking lot. Black Friday limited "hot buys" brings in traffic.

—CATHY AND DALE, 371 FURNITURE

Live events like food and wine etc. to create excitement.

—PJ ORSINI, ORSINI'S

Next-day delivery seven days a week.

—PAUL SHERMAN, SHERMAN'S

Pick two to three zip codes around the store and commit to mailing them every month. This has created more consistent sales and traffic.

—AUSTIN WALLS, WALLS FURNITURE AND MATTRESS

Build a partnership with the local university.

—THI LE, BEDS 4 LESS

Defined who we are and committed to competition amongst ourselves in order to have a different/awesome experience so that customers spread our story.

—STEPHEN PATTERSON, SWEET DREAMS

Daughter appears in TV ads to reinforce family-owned business.

—JIM LYONS, THE FURNITURE GALLERY

Boston Red Sox opening day event, cookout, free food, games, and contests.

—NOREEN, THE FURNITURE GALLERY

Created a recognizable spokeswoman ad campaign continuing with unique ads incorporating the same spokeswoman. Promoting family owned, locally owned.

—THE FURNITURE GALLERY

Flash sale to promote particular bedroom set, short-term sale until "Monday at 5 p.m.," big discounts for a short time.

—KATHY, THE MATTRESS AND BEDROOM OUTLET

Created cool lighting package in store to look like the galaxy. Gets people's attention when they are driving by.

—STACEE CORNETT, CROSSROADS FURNITURE

Painted, changed floor plan, updated lighting, and promoted grand reopening.

—DANIELLE PATRICK, HEAVENLY SLEEP SHOPPE

Loyalty rewards program from Whiz Bang. Ten percent off purchases given back on gift card. Bonus referral program.

—STEVE WILLIAMS, FURNITURE WAREHOUSE

Bring in a single nonperishable item to receive 20 percent off anything in the store. Free in-home consultations, in-store personalized appointment package, room deals, and we will donate your replacement items to charity for you.

—MITCH ROY, INTERNATIONAL FURNITURE WHOLESALERS

Invested in a body-mapping system and committed to TV ad investment for one year. Business is up 50 percent.

—JOE WORRELL

Bring in a yoga and health instructor and do "an evening of creating your best night of sleep." Drawing for free yoga-and-wellness bundle.

—BETHANY SCANLON, OCEAN BREEZE BEDDING

Supported Susan G. Komen breast cancer foundation and promoted donate twenty-five dollars to get a 25 percent discount.

—TONY HOWELL, ROOMS UNLIMITED

Post items at a discount on Facebook Marketplace every day. Consistency.

—TYLER AND JESSICA HARTH, ROOMS UNLIMITED

Facebook promotions and digital ads.

—JACOB NIX, NIX HOME CENTER

Build a campaign around closing on Memorial Day to honor fallen heroes.

—CAITLYN PESL, TEXAS MATTRESS MAKERS

Tax holiday sale...no taxes on sales. Veterans Day sale with reduced prices on discontinued, scratch-and-dent, and special-purchase furniture.

—RAE ADAMS, TONGASS TRADING CO.

Free item with purchase, limited to four hours.

—TONGASS TRADING CO.

Sign holders with sheep mascot with a "take a picture" opportunity.

—MARK CROSS, AMERICA'S MATTRESS

Mattress Man (son) started doing commercials and became a local celebrity.

—PHIL DAMRON, SLEEP-N-AIRE MATTRESS GALLERY

In-store mattress and furniture fundraiser benefiting local middle school on Sunday when the store is normally closed.

—KATY LAW, SWEET DREAMS

Give away mattresses to veterans in need.

—STEVE HOUK, BOISE MATTRESS

Mailers direct to home.

—CHUCK NADER, NADER'S

Get a free steak…don't forget the beef. Get a $300 Omaha Steak Family Pack with any iComfort or Beautyrest Black mattress.

—DUSTIN SCHMIDT, AMERICA'S MATTRESS

My Mattress Sucks contest. Used a local radio station and our Face-book page and had people post pictures of their mattress.

—DUSTIN SCHMIDT, AMERICA'S MATTRESS

Uses his son on all television commercials.

—JUSTIN WILHOIT, SLEEP SOLUTIONS MATTRESS GALLERY

Sign walkers and yard signs.

—JILL THIGPEN, FURNITURE DISTRIBUTORS

We partnered with chiropractors to refer their patients to our stores to be fitted for the right mattress using our patented sleep metric diagnostic process. Patient gets a 5 percent discount and the chiropractor gets a 5 percent referral on the sale.

—BRIAN DAVIS, THE BEDROOM STORE

My daughter and grandson did our commercials giving discount of 1 percent for each can of goods customers brought into the store, up to twenty-five cans.

—MIKE BRUEGGE, BRUEGGE AND CO.

Private letter sale.

—CHAD HAUSMANN, KELSEY FURNITURE

Moonlight sale. Register to win $500 of Christmas cash! Give away gold necklace.

—RITA RIFE AND RICKY OWENS, RIFE'S TV

Tent sale.

—MIKE, PLYMOUTH FURNITURE

Five for five grand opening. Give away five beds…builds great traffic.

—HARRY ROBERTS, MATTRESS FIRM

Car show. Fast cars and food trucks. Create some traffic.

—CRAIG ROBBINS, WALLS FURNITURE AND MATTRESS

Destroy mattresses by burning, cutting, blowing them up…"Destroy High Prices" video. Community coloring contest brought out two hundred people.

—JUSTIN ALLEN, THE MATTRESS STORE

Pillow Palooza with the introduction of the new Serta Hybrid line. Serve hot dogs under a DirecTV tent.

—JOANN LEBEDA, AUDIO-VIDEO PLUS

Buy one, get one free.

—KARL TOBLER, MATTRESS WAREHOUSE

Rode hoverboards when we talked to every customer.

—SETH CARSTENS, MATTRESS SLEEP CENTERS

Online pillow giveaway that had to be picked up in the store.

—DEREK GARZA, NEW BRAUNFELS MATTRESS

More Ideas from Dos Marcos!

You didn't think we'd let you leave without saying one last goodbye, did you? Here are some additional ideas for you to consider. Our parting gifts—our thank you—for spending your time with us and listening to what we have to say.

Themes Galore

Places like Bass Pro Shops and Rainforest Cafe picked a theme and designed the retail experience around it. This draws in people for a unique sensory experience. What could make your business a bigger draw?

Parrots at the Dealership

There was a car dealership that had a parrot that would repeat what customers said. It created word of mouth and made people laugh. Can you find a mascot?

Throwed Rolls and Light Shows

Lambert's near Springfield, Missouri, is the home of "throwed rolls." Instead of simply placing a roll on a guest's plate, a Lambert's employee launches a roll across the crowded room.

Have you ever ridden in a normal Uber? What about a car equipped with a light show that danced along to the beat of the music? Think about this: how can you be known for making something ordinary extraordinary, memorable, and uniquely branded to your business?

Shopping Cruises

Building, buying, or remodeling a house can all be overwhelming. One builder knew about this anxiety and created a shopping cruise. He rented a limo and packed it with snacks and champagne. Then he took couples to all the supply houses and stores they needed to visit to select items for their new home. Can you work with realtors and builders to create a shopping cruise where your store is a port along the path?

"I Like You"

Joe Girard holds the Guinness World Record for most cars sold in a year. One of his best ideas was sending a card that said "I like you" to every customer and noncustomer he ever met. He sent these cards every single month like clockwork.

Duct Tape: From Commodity to Cool

Like envelopes or staplers, tape used to be a boring commodity until Duck Brand duct tape made it cool and creative. They give scholarships to graduating seniors who make their prom outfits from duct tape and give out Duct Tape Dad of the Year awards.

Savannah Bananas Your Business

Go listen to the Jesse Cole interview at MattressPodcast.com. Baseball used to be boring. Just like buying beds. Until Jesse Cole came along. His players dance and go on "dates" during games. Parking penguins. Grandma beauty pageants. A break-dancing first base coach. It's all part of the Savannah Bananas "Fans First" experience. You need to start creating fans, not customers.

Stop, Collaborate, and Listen

Your business is back with a brand-new invention. It's called collaboration. Team up with weight loss centers, gyms and fitness facilities, and chiropractors. Go to bridal shows. Talk with pediatricians (parents need sleep). Meet with veterinarians and talk about pets causing sleep loss. Divorce attorneys! That mattress can't be split.